Guidelines
to Safe Drinking

Guidelines to Safe Drinking

NICHOLAS A. PACE, M.D.

with Wilbur Cross

McGRAW-HILL BOOK COMPANY

New York • St. Louis • San Francisco • Toronto
Hamburg • Mexico

1 2 3 4 5 6 7 8 9 F G R F G R 8 7 6 5 4

ISBN 0-07-048052-4

LIBRARY OF CONGRESS CATALOGING IN PUBLICATION DATA

Pace, Nicholas A.
    Guidelines to safe drinking.
    1. Drinking of alcoholic beverages. 2. Alcoholism—
Prevention. I. Cross, Wilbur. II. Title.
HV5035.P23   1984   362.2'9286   84–11207
ISBN 0–07–048052–4

BOOK DESIGN BY A. CHRISTOPHER SIMON.

Foreword

The subject of alcohol is constantly in the news, whether on radio, on television, or in print. We spend a great deal of time discussing the pros and cons of setting the "legal drinking age" at 18, 19, 20, or 21. We establish tests to determine whether drivers are legally drunk after being stopped by the police. And we are constantly in debate about whether alcohol regulation should be local or federal.

Yet with all the attention given to the legalities and technicalities of drinking and intoxication, we spend very little time *educating* people about alcohol. Many parents, for example, are not aware that a bottle of beer contains as much alcohol as a regular highball. Many individuals are so misinformed about the nature and effects of alcohol that they believe the most absurd myths about it, such as the one that coffee will sober a person up. Or that taking vitamins will prevent hangovers.

Few drinkers really understand what "proof" means as a method of rating alcoholic content. Many people have the notion that if they stick with wines they will never have any drinking problems. Few nonprofessionals can explain *why* drinking on an empty stomach is a poor practice.

Most surprising of all is the fact that the subject of "safe drinking," of moderate, sensible drinking by people who are not alcoholics, is seldom discussed by families or in friendly conversations. It almost seems as though it is considered antisocial or immature to give time and thought to such an idea.

Magazines, newspapers, and books devote endless pages to discussions of diets: How we eat; what we eat; why we eat; and ways in which we can eat more sensibly and with greater attention to our health and well-being. Yet these same publications give little space—if any—to the hows, whats, whys, and wherefores of sensible practices and patterns of drinking.

Alcoholism is constantly in the news—and should be. But let's not forget that the people who are *not* alcoholics or problem drinkers are in the majority, by far. Since even moderate drinkers can become candidates for problem drinking, whether because of personal pressures, changes in lifestyles, or alterations in body chemistry, they need to be alert. They must begin to pay more attention to methods and habits that will keep them from slipping into dangerous drinking habits.

Dr. Nicholas Pace, who developed the concept of this guide to safe drinking, has specialized in the field of alcoholism for many years. He was one of the pioneers in planning and implementing corporate programs to assist employees with drinking problems and get them back to the work force. Over and beyond that, he has been one of the nation's leading advocates of programs to educate the public on alcohol and alcohol abuse. He has long believed that alcoholics and problem drinkers can never touch a drink without getting right back into trouble. But he also believes that all people who drink sociably should be aware of the dangers of alcohol, learn how to drink safely, and be alert to any signs that their drinking may be getting out of hand.

This book on safe-drinking guidelines is long overdue. It should be read by everyone who drinks alcoholic beverages, and kept on the family book shelves as a constant reference.

JOHN DE LUCA
Formerly Director
National Institute on Alcohol Abuse and Alcoholism
Vice President, Director of the Medical Division
Equitable Life Assurance Society of the United States

Contents

Foreword   *vii*
Prologue   *xiii*

1   In the Home—To Drink or Not to Drink   *1*
2   Social Drinking: Parties and Special Occasions   *11*
3   Behind the Wheel: The Road to Disaster   *21*
4   Dining Out on the Town   *33*
5   Drinking and the Business Scene   *45*
6   The Sport and Recreation Environments   *55*
7   Living with an Illness   *67*
8   The Romantic Environment   *79*
9   Alcohol and Youth   *89*
10 Other Settings Where Alcohol Plays a Role   *103*
11 Guidelines   *115*

    Pace Yourself   *116*
    Preventive Thinking   *119*
    Know What You Are Drinking   *121*
    Know How Your Drinking System Functions   *129*
    How to Be Aware of Unsafe Drinking Habits   *136*
    Reasons for Unsafe Drinking   *140*
    How to Form Safe Drinking Habits by Yourself   *145*
    How, Where, and When to Seek Outside Help   *151*

PROLOGUE

A Three-Pronged Weapon Against Unsafe Drinking

During my years of practice as a physician, going back about a quarter of a century, I have had occasion to treat thousands of patients who have had unfortunate experiences with alcoholic beverages. Some of these were one-of-a-kind mishaps caused by alcohol-related accidents, such as automobile collisions, nasty falls, near drownings, and severe cuts or abrasions. Some were short-term drinking disasters relating to people who were drinking too much or a few occasions but who were not real problem drinkers, and who managed to return to more moderate habits and live normal lives. The rest, unfortunately, were patients suffering from the disease of alcoholism, whose only chance of recovery was to abstain permanently, one day at a time.

I have had the good fortune to participate in the planning, establishment, and implementation of a number of alcohol programs for large corporations and have seen tens of thousands of employees rescued from sure disaster. The growth of what we refer to as "EAPs"—Employee Assistance Programs—has been one of the unsung accomplishments of business and industry in the United States, and has gone hand in hand with similar movements on the part of labor and various trade and professional associations that represent employees at all levels.

In the course of my increasing exposure to alcohol-related problems and catastrophes I have, of course, also been exposed to thousands of articles and hundreds of books that have been conceived and written with the idea of helping people with their drinking problems. Most of these have been aimed at problem drinkers, stressing what most people in my field now accept as a basic truth: that alcoholics simply can never drink normally, and that they can recover only by abstaining totally and forever. Very few articles and books, however, have been addressed to people who have developed temporary drinking problems or who feel that for reasons of health and better living they should cut down on their consumption of alcoholic beverages.

It has been of great concern to me that we have been neglecting those people who are on the verge of slipping into unsafe drinking habits—habits that could lead to alcoholism—because their problems have not yet surfaced. The question kept nagging me: How can we alert these people to potential problems?

Over the years, as I treated patients of many kinds and ages, from widely divergent backgrounds, I did what just about any medical doctor does in diagnosing a problem: I asked some questions that would encourage specific answers. *Where* is there discomfort or pain? *When* does it occur? What *kinds* of activities seem to be related to the ailment?

It struck me that this was the kind of diagnosis that was *missing* in books and articles that discussed drinking and were aimed at readers who were not alcoholics, or at least whose drinking habits had not yet deteriorated to the alcoholic stage. So, in conceiving and developing this book on safe drinking, I outlined three separate steps that could help readers to avoid overindulgence and be more aware of warning signals regarding their drinking patterns and activities.

You will find that each chapter is based on a setting, which we refer to as a *scenario*. You can easily identify quickly with one or more of these, depending completely upon the *locations* you are in when you customarily have drinks; the *times* when you are most likely to find yourself with a drink in hand; and the *kinds* of alcoholic beverages you generally consume on these occasions. Thus, if your drinking is largely confined to cocktail parties or drinking at home among other members of your family, and if you practically never entertain or are entertained for business reasons, you focus your attention on the chapters discussing the home and parties. And you simply skip the scenario "Drinking and the Business Scene."

The second ingredient in the formula, if you will, is *preconditioning.* Like so many activities in life, your drinking habits depend upon how you have established your routines, your lifestyle, your motivations—long before you reach the point of involvement. The situation is much like dieting. It is very tough to go on an effective diet unless you have already given serious thought to the times and places where you will be eating regularly, the kinds of limitations you hope to impose on yourself, and the reasons why you must lose a certain number of pounds.

Almost nothing that I have read has devoted much attention to this preconditioning stage, or getting the reader properly synchronized and in tune with the basic objective. We would do well to take a leaf from books on sports and athletics, which almost invariably emphasize the need for proper preconditioning long before engaging in serious exercise. At the very least they stress the value of warming up before tackling any sport so that the body can adjust to the physiological changes that will take place.

The third element in the sequence is *pacing.* It is a curious fact that people may pay a great deal of attention to the types of alcoholic beverages they drink, yet almost never to the amount of *alcohol* they are imbibing on an hourly basis. Part of this dilemma results from the fact that few people actually know how much alcohol a specific drink contains. They seem to know a great deal more about such substances as calories or vitamins or cholesterol than they do about an agent as powerful as ethanol (alcohol). Knowledgeable drinkers, of whom there are all too few, tend to sip and savor drinks, especially those who are connoisseurs of wine or fine Scotches. But the average drinker at a cocktail party will bolt and gulp in between sipping and pay little attention to the end results. A circular drink/drive slide rule to be used as a guide to assist people in determing how to avoid consuming too much alcohol and becoming unsafe drivers is available from the New York State Div. of Alcoholism & Alcohol Abuse, 194 Washington Ave., Albany, NY 12210. It accounts for body weight, number of drinks, and estimated percent of blood alcohol, and indicates dangerous ranges of rate of consumption of alcohol.

The chapters in this book, and the "Guidelines" sections at the end, are laid out in such a way that you can relate your own drinking preferences and habits and patterns to this three-part approach and thus find a better and more reliable way to drinking safely.

Quite simply, the reasons for writing this book are twofold: first, to teach laymen who are nonalcoholics something about alcohol and how to drink alcoholic beverages safely; and, second, to alert them to unsafe drinking habits that could lead to trouble later, and even to the disease of alcoholism.

NICHOLAS A. PACE, M.D.

1

In the Home–
To Drink or Not to Drink

The average residence, whether a small apartment or a comfortable family home in the suburbs, is not likely to have a well-stocked bar with famous brands, racks of imported wines, and a colorful lineup of expensive cordials and liqueurs. Even when considerable expense has been channeled into the construction of a flamboyant imitation of a British pub in the basement family room, the selection of beers, wines, and spirits is likely to be conventional and limited.

Still, a typical dwelling, whatever its size or value on the real estate market, probably contains enough 80-proof spirits, domestic wines, and popular brews to cause a monumental hangover—or worse—for two or three people if they decided to consume the supply during the course of one memorable evening.

Fortunately, most individuals and families are not tempted to such excess, any more than they might impetuously decide to open all the cans and boxes on the pantry shelves and gorge themselves on the contents. The provocative and significant fact, however, is that people know

1

far more about the foods and nonalcoholic beverages they consume than they do about beer, wine, and liquor. This is true of the inhabitants of impressive homes who maintain well-stocked bars, as well as those in more modest circumstances. Wealth and the wherewithal to exercise a liquid taste may provide a semblance of sophistication, but underneath the mask lies a pretty thin understanding of alcohol.

For most of us, the *visual* introduction to alcohol occurs at home, and quite early in life. We vaguely recall as children having seen cans of beer in the refrigerator, wines on the dining room table, or an ice bucket and tray of cocktails when our parents were entertaining. Strangely, few people recall ever *learning* anything much about the contents of those bottles and cans—not until they reached teenage and found their parents suddenly in a frenzy, wondering whether they might be sneaking off with undesirable peers to slug cans of beer or bottles of cheap wine while still well under the legal drinking age.

Ask various adult members of a family what alcohol is and they are more than likely to tell you what it *does* than what it is. Under favorable circumstances, it helps to provide conviviality and good cheer, has a warming influence on old friendships, and is even said to be beneficial to the human body when consumed in moderate amounts. Some will go so far as to say that it helps to relieve personal tensions, stimulates the digestion at the family dinner table, and is said to reduce the chances of heart disease. Many will cite the examples of grandparents and great-grandparents who drank wine or beer or a little whiskey as far back as anyone can remember and lived relatively disease-free lives until dying at the age of 90.

There is enough controversy about the physiological benefits of alcohol so that only a pessimist would try to puncture the illusion of alcohol as something of a cure-all when consumed in spare doses.

But ask any of these people what alcohol *is* and they will flounder helplessly over a definition that is probably based on myth anyway.

When we refer to the alcohol in alcoholic beverages, we are talking about *ethyl alcohol,* or *ethanol.* Despite the exorbitant costs of some popular drinks and brands, ethanol is one of the world's most ancient waste products. It is the substance that is left over from yeast after the latter has been used for the fermentation of vegetable sugars. Furthermore, it has the dubious honor of carrying a load of calories yet at the same time being almost totally nonnutritional.

If you don't cringe at the thought of having cave people as ancestors, you can picture your hairy forebears discovering the stuff that was later to make the cocktail party and the business lunch a little less civilized a million years later. They probably encountered alcohol first in the form of naturally fermented fruit juice, the first and crudest vintage of wine. Later it appeared as mead, a distinctive ritual drink for the ancient Greeks, but a concoction to be avoided by the bees who made the honey from whence it came.

Ethanol was no less a by-product when it originated in the chemical decomposition of grains and formed the first bitter and all but unpalatable beers. It took the ancient Egyptians thousands of years to perfect beers that could be considered beverages rather than fertilizers. But if their pharaohs could tackle the building of pyramids without losing their minds, it stands to reason that creating malt beverages must have been a relatively minor challenge.

Ethanol tends to be misleading. Like carbohydrates and fats, it can be readily absorbed into the body from the gastrointestinal tract. Unlike them, however, it is not effectively stored in the tissues. Quite the contrary, it often depletes the body of certain elements that have already been stored in the tissues. It punishes people who have overindulged for example, by robbing them of B-complex vitamins, stealing vitamin A from the liver, and sometimes doing the same with vitamin C. Where does it hide these stolen treasures? No one knows.

Ethanol poses little threat for the moderate drinker, yet it has to be recognized for what it most importantly is: the *intoxicating agent* in alcoholic beverages. In its natural form it is a clear, colorless liquid with almost no odor. Its social virtue is that it mixes easily with water in all proportions, and for that matter just about any other liquid, thick or thin.

What Are Alcoholic Beverages?

The most common, down through the ages and in all human civilizations, are the wines, produced by the fermentation of the juice of ripe grapes and other fruits. Common table wines consist of about 12 percent alcohol by volume if they are dry (containing very little sugar) and 15 percent if they have enough sugar to be considered sweet. Aperitif and dessert wines, like sherry and port, may range from 18 to 22 percent in alcoholic content. This may explain why some of those tiny, snow-haired grandmothers who "don't drink anything but an occasional glass of sherry" can sometimes look so smugly beyond the cares of the immediate household.

Champagne and other sparkling wines earn their reputation as "party drinks for special occasions," not from their alcohol content, which is generally around 12 percent, but from the carbon dioxide gas in their content. The gas, developed naturally in fine champagnes and injected in the cheaper brands, has the effect of hastening the action whereby the ethanol is absorbed into the body.

Ale and beer are brewed from malt mixtures that are produced from moist grains of barley to which dried hops are added. Fermentation is as important as it is in the making of wines, and continues slowly during the brewing process. The resulting liquid is clarified and carbonated before being put into kegs, bottles, or cans for shipment. Popular brands of American beer contain 4 or 5 percent alcohol by volume. Beers from Europe and the orient are generally higher. Ale is usually stronger than beer, ranging as high as 8 percent. Two related products are porter and stout, dark-colored ales that contain more sugar and tend to be bitter in taste. They also may contain as much as 8 percent alcohol.

Few people seem to realize it (or else want to fool themselves), but the alcohol in ales and beers is *ethanol,* the very same as that found in whiskey or vodka or gin.

Why should we be in a completely different ball park then when we look at the roster of what we call *distilled spirits?* Are they all that much more potent? The answer is both yes and no, qualified by "it depends. . . ."

Ounce for ounce, whiskeys, rums, gins, vodkas, and other common distilled spirits *are* more potent than wines and beers. Their alcohol (ethanol) content is classified by *proof* rather than *percentage by volume.* The proof is exactly twice the percentage. Thus, an 80-proof blended whiskey contains 40 percent alcohol. Most of the common brands range from 80 to 100 proof. Special imports may range as high as 150, while pure grain alcohol hits the top at 200 proof because it has been distilled until it is nothing but 100 percent alcohol.

The making of whiskey requires complex processes of fermentation and distillation. Even so, it usually ends up as a raw product that has to be treated further and aged to give it the proper color and flavor. Bourbon, which is made largely from corn and some rye, is often aged in charred oak barrels, which give it a distinctive flavor. Scotch derives its smoky taste from malt that has been roasted over peat fires.

The great differentials in the making of various alcoholic beverages suggests an important truth: Safe drinking is more than a matter of *how much* you drink. It is also a real question of *what* you drink, *where* you drink, *how* you drink, and, above all, *how your body metabolizes or handles* what you drink. Alcohol is absorbed directly into the bloodstream from the stomach, but not at the same rate for all kinds of drinks. For some reason, perhaps because of the many other substances in its makeup, wine is absorbed much more slowly into the bloodstream than are distilled beverages. The same is true of beer. But when you drink whiskey, the alcohol is absorbed very quickly and produces a more marked effect upon you and your behavior. Once alcohol is in the bloodstream, there is nothing you can do to clear the alcohol from your system. Nature takes its course. The body metabolizes the alcohol at the rate of three-quarters of an ounce of pure alcohol per hour. Plunging into a cold shower, drinking a pint of black coffee, swallowing a large dose of vitamins, exercising violently— none of these mythical cures accomplishes anything, outside of perhaps making you sick or exhausted.

The body rids itself of alcohol by oxidizing it. Fat and carbohydrates can be processed by almost all of the body's tissues in a healthy manner. But not alcohol. Some 95% of it *must* be oxidized in the liver, the body's main chemical plant and the one organ that contains the kinds of enzymes necessary for this function. The remaining 5% of the alcohol is excreted, unchanged, through the kidneys and lungs. Consequently, anyone who drinks heavily is automatically committing his liver to an overload of work, sometimes with considerable harm. The liver already has plenty of work to take care of, let alone processing alcohol, since it is the primary organ in the synthesis of proteins and the neutralization of foreign substances, including other kinds of drugs.

Effect on Individuals

For families who enjoy alcoholic beverages in moderation, individually or together, drinking may have a place in the home in a number of ways. Alcohol is at its best when imbibed as part of a regular meal and as a food in itself. Wine and beer (but not distilled spirits) are much like fats and carbohydrates in what they contribute to the metabolic process in building energy. But these are naked calories and, as such, cannot be stored.

Some feel that alcoholic beverages, including a cocktail that is properly mixed and not sweet, can stimulate the appetite before meals. So-called aperitifs, like dry sherry, Dubonnet, or vermouth, are excellent for this purpose. When it comes to mixed drinks that are made with hard liquor, however, most amateur bartenders tend to have a heavy hand with the whiskey, vodka, or gin. The resultant drink may deaden, rather than enhance, the appetite. A good rule of thumb is to serve premeal drinks that contain no more than 25 percent alcohol by volume and that are consumed within 30 or 40 minutes of the meal. If you go beyond these limits, your appetite will diminish—which is usually what happens with the average "Happy Hour" at home.

Moderation is always the key because—no matter what other factors come into an evaluation of drinking, pro and con—alcohol can play havoc with family diets. A single ounce of pure alcohol ends up in the body as about 170 calories. One authority on diets likened this caloric richness to that of a dozen raw oysters, a broiled lamb chop, or a baked potato, yet without contributing any nutrition at all.

Parents who elect to serve alcoholic beverages in the

home in a manner that will provide mutual enjoyment and establish safe drinking habits for all members of the family sometimes overlook one important fact: individual responses to the consumption of alcohol vary widely. A young woman who weighs a mere 105 pounds will feel the effects of a cocktail or glass of wine more quickly and emphatically than, say, her father who tips the scales at 210 and is more accustomed to drinking. A large body tends to "dilute" the alcohol ingested more than does a small body. The effect is somewhat similar to pouring an ounce of dye into two glass jars, holding one quart and half a gallon of water respectively. The resulting color of the latter will be weaker in tone than the former.

Other factors besides weight that control the immediate effect of drinks on people are the state of their health, both physical and emotional; tensions and pressures relating to jobs or personal relationships; financial and other economic demands; dramatic changes in one's life or lifestyle; and—let's face it—an individual's overall experience with the drinking of alcoholic beverages.

This all brings up the question of whether families should tolerate, even encourage, drinking in the home. Why make it available and thus tempt young people to get into bad habits? Those in favor point out that children are going to be exposed to alcohol in one way or another no matter what the customs may be at home, and with increasing frequency as they grow older. They will see adult parties in progress, will encounter people in public places who have overindulged, and will sooner or later be pressured by their peers into sipping beer or wine or something harder. Nevertheless, while drinking should surely be discussed, it should not be *encouraged* among young family members.

In many countries families serve alcoholic beverages, traditionally and culturally to members of all ages in a perfectly relaxed and natural way. Youngsters in Spain,

Italy, and China, for example, are accustomed to tasting and sipping wine when they are quite young. Jewish families serve wines in moderate amounts. Since the wines tend to be sweet and heavy, young people seldom overindulge, and become accustomed to thinking of wine as something that is consumed in small quantities.

Many families in America, by contrast, are hypercritical and self-conscious about alcohol. It is difficult, if not impossible, to regard alcohol as a normal, natural substance. Why should this be? The answer lies in a complex amalgam of opinions and viewpoints and reactions. Alcohol appears in many dramatic and highly unrealistic guises. It is the "hero" of the popular beer commercials, ranked on a par with star quarterbacks and home-run sluggers. It is the "villain" who has caused the downfall of bright young executives and formerly adoring and supportive parents. It is the symbol of guilt, passed down to trouble us from generations of Puritans and axe-wielding prohibitionists. It is the ever-present enigma that splits academic researchers into opposing camps and challenges the scientific community to define accurately what effects it really has on the human system, physiologically and psychologically.

In the confusing environment of advertising copy, grabby commercials, scary editorials, and public gatherings of concerned citizens, it is little wonder that the image of alcohol is blurred in the minds of so many.

PACE YOURSELF !

For more detailed counsel on safe drinking in the home, refer to the following sections in the "Guidelines" chapter of this book:

A. Pace Yourself
    Sections 1 to 3

B. Preventive Thinking
   Sections 1 to 7
C. Know What You Are Drinking
   Sections 1 to 15
D. Know How Your Drinking System Functions
   Sections 1 to 4, 13
E. How to Be Aware of Unsafe Drinking Habits
   Sections 3 to 5, 7

2

Social Drinking: Parties and Special Occasions

"If I had to come up with an unhealthy drinking situation," wrote one of the world's outstanding specialists on alcoholism, "I would have created the American cocktail party."

This usually noisy, sometimes garish social institution does indeed have all the ingredients necessary for alcoholic disaster. The guests drink more than they should in order to achieve a kind of instant friendship with strangers; the host doubles the proportion of liquor per drink in order to offset any deficiencies in the setting or the attendance; and the timing is such that almost everyone has arrived with an empty stomach, which will be little alleviated by the passing of pretty platters of thimble-sized hors d'oeuvres.

Gulping drinks becomes almost compulsive at such affairs, because what else does one do when standing self-consciously alone amidst a sea of faces, or when there is an uncomfortable pause in a conversation that has been losing out to the rising noise level anyway?

Drinking in a private residence under the label of a

11

"party" or similar social occasion is not entirely a matter of degree, as many people are inclined to think. Many factors are involved that have a bearing on the way alcohol affects the guests in general, individuals in particular, and the ones who are hosting the party. Although people are supposedly invited to have a relaxing period of fun and camaraderie, certain pressures exist that are not present, say, when a family group is enjoying wine at dinner.

Why, then, has the typical American cocktail party gotten so preposterously out of hand? Ideally, a good party is one where the guests feel mellow and relaxed, yet no one gets drunk, and where people are likely to remember the occasion as one that was fun and their hosts as people who were both hospitable and considerate.

It would probably take a major social revolution to redesign the cocktail party so that it is civilized and respectable, yet totally enjoyable. Short of undertaking such a measure (which could never get through Congress!) the next best solution is to inform people how to enjoy the meager benefits of this kind of party while avoiding the risks.

That's easy—PACE YOURSELF!

Easier said than done, but there actually are two sets of criteria that work, one for the *guests* and one for the *hosts.* We'll tackle the guests first, since they predominate, numerically and vociferously.

The first criterion is to make sure that you are in *good condition,* just as though you were readying yourself for the playing field, which, in a manner of speaking, is just what you are doing. Make sure you've had enough rest, are in reasonably good health, and aren't knotted with tensions and apprehensions because of your job, romantic relationships, or the miserable fluctuations of the stock market. If you are tense, besieged with a migraine headache, or feeling that the whole world is against you, better to send regrets and not go at all than to go and regret that you did.

The second imperative is to take a kindly and considerate look (theoretically speaking) at your stomach. When did you feed it last with a substantial meal? Since most cocktail parties are scheduled for "sixish" or later, especially on weekends, the likelihood is that you'll arrive some six hours after having finished lunch. Alcohol goes to work with a kind of fiendish fury on an empty stomach, where there is no food to slow down its quick transition into the bloodstream. If this is the case, don't count on finding a hearty display of food that you can gobble unobtrusively when arriving on location. Play it safe by treating your tummy to something that will line it effectively. A thick peanut butter and jelly sandwich will do if there is nothing more substantial in the refrigerator.

Cultivate the fine art of *dawdling*. Once you arrive at the scene and are suddenly thrust from the relative silence of the exterior world into the echoing social clatter, use your skills to delay the inevitable question, "What'll you have to drink?" This can be done by prolonging the temporary disposal of hat, coat, gloves, boots, umbrella, or other impedimenta; by admiring pictures on the wall; or by spotting someone you know well and using the delaying tactic of intense conversation on some issue that will take awhile to resolve. With luck, you can kill 10 minutes before you are led (or pushed) towards the bar. By then, your hosts or the help will probably have forgotten you anyway and zeroed in on some other recent arrival.

The greatest hurdle simply has to be that moment when you finally arrive at the bar, or are all but ordered to announce what suits your pleasure in the way of a drink. What suits *your* pleasure may not be exactly what the hosts have in mind. They have mixed a trayful of the drink for which they have earned a reputation: A Jamaican Zilly with three kinds of rum. You absolutely *must* have one! Under such circumstances, it's not always easy for you to order the drink recommended in the next paragraph.

If you intend to remain at the party for the duration, or a reasonable part of it, your first drink should be nonalcoholic or light in alcohol. A *spritzer* is a sensible (and increasingly acceptable) choice. If mixed properly, it will contain half white wine and half club soda, and be served in a tall, attractive glass. Even an empty stomach will tolerate a spritzer, if it is sipped slowly and you have a chance to nibble hors d'oeuvres that are more than flakes and fluff.

No matter what the circumstances, you should be able to refuse a drink without feeling uncomfortable, though you may be in the grip of one of those hosts of the "Old School," who feels that a cocktail party isn't a party without martinis, manhattans, and daiquiris aplenty. The best approach is *honesty,* if only because it discombobulates the host who has all the answers to would-be teetotalers. Smile disarmingly, say that you aren't drinking today, or express profuse thirst and the desire for a soda before you even begin to contemplate serious drinking. It may be the host's party, but it's *your* stomach!

People who have trouble refusing without blushing and find themselves with an unwanted drink in hand can be pardoned for taking this emergency measure: making one's way casually to the bathroom and pouring most of the beverage down the sink.

Don't be afraid of pressure. Most people who give parties are trying hard to be sociable and want to give the impression of offering total hospitality. Once you have asserted yourself, they are usually turning to the next nearest guest anyway and you can relax and seek out a fellow conversationalist who seems more interested in the people in the room than the proof on the bottles.

The next worthwhile goal is to become a selective nibbler. If the party is one of those peanuts-and-potato-chips affairs, you are unlikely to find much in the way of sustenance unless you have happened to put a candy bar in pocket or purse before arriving. But if you can locate sandwiches, cheeses, or casserole dips you're in luck. Your stomach will take more kindly to alcohol, even should you go on to a cocktail or highball.

If you have an experimental turn of mind and like to try new things, confine your exploration to food rather than alcoholic beverages. Some concoctions can be dynamite, especially if your friendly hosts consider themselves inventive and/or innovative. It's a good idea, too, when ordering purely conventional drinks to spell out the proportions you want in any kind of mixture. As you may have noticed, hired bartenders seem obsessed with the idea that their reputation depends on how many jiggers or "splashes" they can inject into a cocktail or highball without overflowing the glass.

One final word of counsel for guests: When accepting an invitation to a cocktail party, always try to anticipate realistically *how long* it will last. The invitation that reads "6 to 8" can often be interpreted as "Come anytime and stay until midnight." It's not considered polite to exact specific information from your hosts-to-be beforehand, such as length, number of guests expected, and kinds of food that will be served. You can sometimes get around this, however, by making a leading comment when you phone your acceptance.

"It sounds like fun, and just at the right time because we had planned to go out to dinner around eight. . . ."

Or, "We may be a little late because John has an appointment that will keep him until almost seven. . . ."

The reaction at the other end of the line will oftentimes alert you to the fact that substantial foods are to be served or that the party is expected to go on long past the time indicated on the invitation. Once you have determined as much as possible about the length and nature of the party, do yourself a favor and decide in advance *when you are going to leave.* Once you have made this decision, stick to your intentions. No statement in our language has been the cause of more regrets the day after than "I'll stay around and just have one more. . . ."

If you are coerced into staying for whatever reason, do yourself an even greater favor and subsist from that point on hot coffee or soft drinks, instead of beer, wine, or hard liquor.

Emphatic Hints for Host and Hostess

People who like to entertain despise and detest advice, especially if it has anything to do with conduct and behavior. The are open to creative suggestions of all kinds and may spend hours poring through the colorful magazines in search of ideas for food, beverages, decorations, and serving. But let some well-meaning expert toss a carefully conceived "do" or "don't" their way and the reaction is the same as if they had been aimed at with a shotgun. Despite the futility of it all, here are some points that must be pondered by every considerate host and hostess planning a party at which alcoholic beverages will be served.

Always place *nonalcoholic beverages* on the bar or in a place that is as conspicuous as that devoted to the alcoholic ones. These should be offered and served attractively, in proper glasses and with lime and other garnishments, if appropriate. In addition to various sodas, you can now obtain an increasing number of "light" wines that contain 7 to 9 percent alcohol instead of the usual 12 to 15, and some new types that contain *no alcohol at all.* These are not imitations but wines that have been fermented and brewed in traditional ways and then *dealcoholized.* The alcohol is removed, down to less than 0.5 percent, leaving the full taste and body of the original.

You can actually be quite creative in preparing and serving nonalcoholic drinks that are tasty and appealing, using attractive glasses and pitchers, properly iced. One innovative hostess, Jane Brandt, has written a recipe book, *Drinks without Liquor,* * which tells you how to make party drinks with names like Orange Nog Supreme (juices and spices), Witchie's Stew (orange juice, spices, and cider), Hawaiian Coffee Punch (coffee, soda, and pineapple), Tropical Cucumber (lemon, lime, cucumber), and Strawberry Slim (strawberries, club soda, yogurt). Your selections can range all the way from sweet and fruity energizers to low-calorie quenchers and hot nogs for winter holidays. The author also suggests ways of coloring ice and adding other festive touches so that the drinks really have a festive look as well as flavor.

You can obtain plenty of "light" beers, whose alcohol content is about 3 percent, and quite a few brands that, like the new wines, have been dealcoholized. Experts who have conducted taste tests have been very complimentary about several brands of both beer and wine.

Whether you are serving dinner later or not, offer two or three types of hors d'oeuvres that are substantial enough to assuage empty stomachs and slow the absorption of alcohol into the bloodstream. These should be passed around often, and particularly to individuals and groups who seem to be imbibing cocktails or other drinks containing hard liquor.

Whatever you do, don't get the reputation of being a host or hostess who forces drinks on guests and serves dinner very late!

* Jane Brandt, *Drinks without Liquor,* Workman Publishing Company, New York, 1983.

Shy away from serving *double-strength* drinks or those that contain a variety of liquors and are considered potent. Some people actually keep count of their drinks and are quite aware of their limits. So if the three drinks you give them are actually equivalent to four (or more) you may inadvertently be leading them into depths beyond where they intended to go. You may do this out of a sense of generosity, or the fear that guests will laugh at your idea of what a good drink is. But actually you are being inconsiderate, if not downright rude. If you have hired a bartender or have asked a friend or relative to assist at the bar, make sure they really know how to mix the right proportions and not end up with "bombs."

Be conservative in the matter of *refills*. Here again, most hosts make the mistake of overdoing it, eager to make sure that they uphold the reputation of being hospitable and generous. One experienced host says it helps him always to keep in mind, not what his guests are thinking about him during the party, but what they are going to say to themselves the next morning: "Oh, my aching brain! John is sure no friend of mine or he wouldn't have pressured me into those last two drinks!"

The really hospitable host ranks several other activities ahead of the job of simply serving drinks. One is to make people at ease (which drinks are supposed to do but often don't), to circulate and introduce people who don't know each other, and to break up the usual deadlock when two people seem to have run out of conversation but don't know how to back off tactfully. Another important function is to regulate activities in such a way that the party will phase out at the right time and guests will leave contentedly, with no feeling that they have been pushed out the door. This maneuver takes considerable skill, far more than maintaining a well-stocked bar.

Last, and certainly not least, the hosts are responsible

for seeing that any one who *has* imbibed too quickly or too freely gets home safely, whether it requires a personal escort, hiring a cab, or talking the problem guest into staying overnight and sleeping it off. Most critical of all is the case of the person who has had one too many and is insisting on driving home, with or without passengers.

You can figure that it will require 1 hour for *each* drink to be metabolized before that person is fit to drive. No matter what you have to do, take positive action to see that a person who is drunk does not get behind the wheel. (This situation is covered in detail in Chapter 3.)

Do you have plenty of black coffee to give people who have been drinking too much? The only way it will do any good is if you give it to the Big Drinkers *in place of* the last drink or two, not afterward. While coffee is a great substitute for alcohol, it has absolutely no power to sober up a drunk or alleviate the hangover that has already been triggered.

Offering hot coffee early on during a cocktail party will earn considerate hosts the thanks and respect of their guests. It is surprising to see how many people actually make a beeline for the coffee urn when it is placed on a conveniently located table. It's well worth the trouble.

PACE YOURSELF !

For more detailed references on social drinking, parties, and alcohol, refer particularly to the following sections in the "Guidelines" chapter of this book.

A. Pace Yourself
   Sections 1 to 6
B. Preventive Thinking
   Sections 1 to 7

D. Know How Your Drinking System Functions
    Sections 11 to 13
E. How to Be Aware of Unsafe Drinking Habits
    Sections 2, 6, 7
F. Reasons for Unsafe Drinking
    Sections 1, 2, 8
G. How to Form Safe Drinking Habits by Yourself
    Sections 1 to 5

3

Behind the Wheel:
The Road to Disaster

Who are the drivers who cause accidents as a result of drinking (excluding those who are problem drinkers or alcoholics and who must be considered from a different viewpoint altogether)? For the most part, they are people who do not understand what alcohol does to the body and whose judgment and reflexes have been impaired far more seriously than they honestly realized.

They are also the victims of myths, such as the prevalent one that a steaming mug of black coffee will neutralize the effects of alcohol. Or that if they douse their heads in cold water and wait 60 minutes, they will automatically be sober enough to get behind the wheel. Some, too, are the drivers who become super cautious when they have indulged too much and think that if they creep along at 25 miles per hour and shun the turnpikes they will avoid calamity.

To understand why drinking and driving are so often the most fatal of mixtures, you have to know something about the effect of alcohol on the human body. Once in the body, alcohol is absorbed rapidly from the mucous membranes of the mouth, stomach, and intestines. Unlike other foods and beverages, it does not have to be digested before being absorbed, which is why its effects are felt so quickly after a drink is taken.

Because alcohol is carried first to the brain, it has a quick negative effect on coordination and the ability to think clearly and react instantaneously.

Although alcohol can enter the bloodstream directly from the stomach, its absorption is most rapid from the upper portion of the small intestine. The stomach can actually delay the process if it contains food, the speed of the action of the delay depending to a large extent on the type and amount of what the stomach contains. That is why it is always good practice to eat before drinking, and *while* drinking if you are at a party or other social event for a long time.

Weight is a definite factor in the degree to which alcohol affects a person, all other factors (such as health, state of mind, and freedom from tension) being equal. A young woman weighing 115 pounds, for example, can be seriously impaired after consuming three 12-ounce cans of beer during a 2-hour period. A football player weighing 230 pounds could drink six cans before reaching the same degree of impairment, but would be legally drunk if he consumed seven during that same period of time. In most states, the operator of a motor vehicle is judged by law to be intoxicated when the percent of alcohol in the blood is at or above the .10 level. Never use the legal limit, however, as a standard for determining your own drinking capacity. The hazards to you, your health, and your relationships with other people may be far below that legal danger zone.

Time is also a key factor, not only the period during which drinks are consumed but also the amount of time that has passed between the last drink and getting behind the wheel of a car. It will take a man of 150 or 160 pounds at least one hour to metabolize an ounce of 90-proof hard liquor. If he has consumed five times that amount then his body requires five hours to rid itself of the alcohol.

One of the reasons why drinking is so dangerous in situations requiring clear thinking and quick reflexes is that the chemical formula for alcohol is very close to that of ether. The effect on the drinker involves the same kind of anesthetic action. *That is why drinking was responsible for half of all* highway traffic fatalities, or an average over the past decade of 25,000 per year, not to mention some half million alcohol-related injuries.

Without too much effort, you can find all kinds of horrible statistics about death and mayhem on the highway that can be directly traced to alcoholic beverages. But these facts tend to be meaningless to most people. They want to understand the personal implications and how they are affected.

Look at it this way: You drive down to the local pub with a couple of friends and during a friendly sojourn of about an hour and a half consume three beers or two highballs containing a total of 3 ounces of whiskey. Can you drive home safely? Legally, you can. The amount of alcohol in your blood is only about 0.05 percent. But here's what those modest little drinks have done to you, physically and mentally:

Your eye reaction is markedly slower.

Peripheral vision is decreased.

Visual acuity is reduced by as much as one-third, or comparable to wearing dark glasses while driving at night.

The recovery time for headlight glare is much longer, ranging from 10 to 30 seconds, depending upon the individual.

Your reaction time is slowed from 15 to 25 percent.

Judgments about distance and speed are faulty.

Your attention to detail lags and you are more likely to

talk and relate to what's going on inside the car (a kind of carry-over from the period of convivial drinking in the bar, or elsewhere).

You are more than likely to have a false sense of your competency behind the wheel.

Precautions are curbed and you may tend to be slightly belligerent towards other drivers, who do not seem to be giving you proper right of way.

Overall, your total driving impairment is likely to range from 25 percent to almost 50 percent, in terms of your physical and mental responses, your reaction time, and your ability to detect unexpected hazards. Few people realize it, but drivers have to make about 100 decisions for every mile of driving on the open road, and more than twice that many per mile when driving in urban traffic. That leaves a lot of room for error for the driver who is not completely in control of his car and his senses. As a report from the National Council on Alcoholism translated this in terms of statistics: "The drinking driver is 25 times more likely to have an accident than a sober driver."

Impact on Youth

It is a sobering fact that *drunk driving is the leading single cause of death among young people in the age range from 16 to 24.* That is one reason why *insurance rates in these brackets are often much higher than what they are for people 25 and older.* Is it because young people are drinking more and more, turning perhaps from the hard drugs to alcohol? In some cases this is true. However, the reasons are much more complicated. And they are almost contradictory. It seems on the surface to be quite illogical that healthy young people in their teens and twenties who have quick reflexes and are physically adept should fare so tragically on the highway.

Part of the answer to the puzzle lies in the fact that

young adults lack three essential qualities for driving: *patience, judgment,* and *experience.* Drivers in their teens and twenties get into trouble on these counts more often than adults even when they have not touched a drop of alcohol. When they drink, the margins of error are magnified more than they are for most older drivers. They get itchy waiting in line for a light, and irritated if stuck behind a truck or a slow-moving oldster. They may misjudge the distance available for passing. Alcohol makes many young drivers think that their cars have far more power reserve than is possible. Or that they can stop on a dime. Or that their passengers will respect their daring if they take a few chances. Result: unnecessary mayhem.

More than any other age group, young people who are driving to and from a party must learn how to pace themselves and their activities with great personal care and understanding. They can accomplish this kind of pacing very readily and effectively in sports and physical activities of all kinds—so why not when socializing?

One field of knowledge has been greatly, if not totally overlooked in our educational system. It should be given in high school, in college, in graduate school, and in continuing education curricula. The subject: Party Giving I: Survival.

The proposed course would be light on the frivolities of entertaining and the details of clever menus and decorations. It would focus instead on methods for assuring the health and welfare of the guests at social events where alcohol is to be consumed and would consist of the following essentials:

Part I: Before and during the Party

1. Always serve food with alcoholic beverages. High-protein foods such as cheese and meats are especially desirable because they remain in the stomach longer.

Hard-boiled eggs, deviled or pickled, are usually welcome, along with Swedish meatballs, broiled chicken livers, and assorted raw vegetables with an accompanying dip.

2. Have plenty of nonalcoholic beverages prominently available at the bar.

3. Provide several jiggers at the bar, so mixed drinks can be easily measured. Self-measuring 1-ounce spouts are also available for use on liquor bottles.

4. If you serve an alcoholic punch, make it mild and with a *non*carbonated base. Alcohol is absorbed by the body much faster when combined with a carbonated mixer such as ginger ale or club soda. Fruit juices or tea are preferable bases and combine well with the alcoholic ingredient.

5. Never force drinks on your guests. Take the opposite tack and get people involved in activities other than drinking, as much as you tactfully can. Oftentimes, guests hold drinks just to be polite and have something to do with their hands, and the last thing they want is for the hosts to keep watching their levels of consumption.

6. Stop serving alcohol about an hour before the party is to end. You don't have to make a big deal of closing the bar. Simply remove the alcoholic beverages unobtrusively and substitute coffee, tea, and other nonalcoholic liquids. When the guests are young people, they are likely to be delighted if you bring out small pizzas, quiches, desserts, or fruit.

7. During the party, and particularly near the end, keep your eyes open for young guests who are drinking too much or too quickly. Try to engage them in conversation to slow their drinking, or have one of their peers undertake the job. Offer food or coffee—but remember that these things will only serve as *substitutes* for liquor and will have absolutely no sobering effect.

Part II: After the Party

If a guest has had too much to drink and nonetheless intends to drive home, there are six steps that you as the host can—and must, if necessary—take:

1. Make the suggestion that you drive him or her home. Arrangements for picking up the car can be made the next day.
2. Invite your guest to stay overnight—despite any inconvenience it may cause. Better a small discomfort than a major catastrophe.
3. If he or she is beyond reason and insisting on driving, try to take the car keys away. You'll get a lot of resentment, but that's the least of your worries.
4. Physically restrain him to the best of your ability without causing an outright fight. Try to anticipate this far enough ahead of time to enlist the aid of a peer who is strong and sensible.
5. Call a taxi and have your guest taken home, preferably with an escort.
6. If all five of these measures fail, you have only one alternative left: Phone the police. Distasteful though this may seem, the sight of a police officer may be the only thing that will shock the person into acting more rationally. Usually, the police are friendly, though firm, and will try to be helpful in making other arrangements.

Over the years, many different approaches have been tried during major efforts to reduce the number of drunks who take to the road. These measures include road blocks to check the condition of *all* drivers along a given stretch of highway over a period of several hours; mandatory jail sentences and stiffer fines; license suspensions; alcohol rehabilitation programs; and higher legal drinking ages in each state.

The manufacturers of automobiles, in conjunction with government agencies, have experimented with ingenious devices to prevent alcohol-impaired drivers from starting cars to begin with. Some of these have involved a complex series of numbers that have to be correctly aligned before the ignition can be turned on. The theory, of course, is that some one who has had too much alcohol cannot complete the sequence in the right order. A more refined unit, developed by General Motors, works by having the driver align two indicators. If this is not completed, the car sounds an alarm, alerting pedestrians and other motorists to the impaired condition of the driver.

The *emotional* approach to drunk driving has been partially effective, largely because it has forced individuals to think for a moment and reevaluate their own habits on the highway. One effective organization, for example, is MADD—Mothers Against Drunk Drivers. It was founded by a mother whose daughter was struck while walking to a church carnival early one afternoon. Her body was hurled 120 feet through the air when a drunk driver lost control of his car and swerved off the road. She died less than an hour later. MADD has been instrumental in promoting legislation to toughen anti-drunk-driving laws and has enlisted the aid of communities across the country.

Most of these countermeasures have helped—up to a point. But they are effective only when they bring about changes in personal attitudes and understanding. The answer lies in developing more practical and realistic education programs so that individuals discover what alcohol is all about and learn how to cope with it—literally to *pace themselves* whenever they drink.

Pacing requires the methods already discussed, such as sipping drinks slowly, alternating alcoholic with nonalcoholic beverages, selecting light drinks instead of strong ones, and setting a limit. Equally important, it involves the technique of *preconditioning* yourself, so that your judgment while in full command of your faculties carries over into situations when you are drinking. It is almost like a reflex action that has been programmed into your brain— like not touching a hot burner on the kitchen range.

Give some thought in advance to the social affair or other event you'll be attending where alcoholic beverages are going to be served. What will you start off with? What will you switch to? How will you respond when your host or hostess tries to pressure you into another drink, or a different kind of drink? At what point will you decide that you have had enough? Who are the people you'll be associating with most at the party and what are their drinking habits, good or bad?

Most importantly, what limits are you setting if you have to drive? Or what would you do if you are a passenger in someone else's car and the driver turns out to have had too much to drink?

This is *preconditioning,* anticipating everything that will, or might, have to do with alcohol consumption. People who are normal drinkers under most circumstances often complain that they don't seem to have much control over the situations that develop at a party. They become "victims of circumstances" most often when the party is over and it is time to drive (or be driven) home. What really happens is that they plan poorly to begin with and later find themselves without any alternate plan of action.

The Accident Prone

It is a well-documented fact that drinking and automobile accidents go hand in hand. The problem is paralleled in other fields of activity as well. Studies have shown, for instance, that alcoholics are seven times more likely than nonalcoholics to meet with fatal accidents of all kinds. These include an astonishing number of deaths from fire and asphyxiation because of alcohol-related carelessness (such as falling asleep with lighted cigarettes or leaving flammable materials too near the burners of a kitchen range).

Boating accidents and drownings are often associated with the overconsumption of alcoholic beverages. People not only mishandle the equipment or misjudge the power of the motor responding to their command, but run out of fuel, make poor decisions, lose their way, or otherwise place themselves in dangerous situations. Overindulgence tends to make people foolhardy (it seems "brave" at the time!). They take chances that they never would dream of risking when cold sober, extend themselves far beyond their limit, or have a false sense of security in their capabilities or equipment.

There has been an increase in alcohol-related accidents involving other forms of transportation, too, from motorcycles to light planes, snowmobiles, sailboats, and—more recently—cross-country skiing.

Drinking has been pinpointed as a factor in accidents in the home, such as falling off ladders, getting cut with knives and other sharp instruments, and being subjected to various kinds of serious bumps and bruises. The advent of all kinds of power equipment for the yard, such as automatic lawn mowers, hedge trimmers, and tree saws, has opened up a whole new area of opportunities for disaster. The amateur gardener or gentleman farmer who likes to guzzle beer while operating these expensive playthings may well end up cutting something more delicate and painful than fibers and wood.

The negative effects of alcohol on the mental processes has led to countless fires, scaldings, and serious burns, both outdoors and indoors. Nothing mixes more dangerously than the alcohol in a strong cocktail on the terrace and the alcohol in the nearby outdoor grill.

Statistics indicate that alcohol is a direct factor in more than 50 percent of all accidental deaths—whether on the highway, in fires, on the water, or in falls both inside and outside the home. In such cases the victims seldom have been known to have oriented themselves about the potential of alcohol and probably never have anticipated the dangers of mixing alcohol with what otherwise might have been perfectly normal pursuits.

In summation, the best slogan ever coined was: "If you drive, don't drink. If you drink, don't drive! This advice can apply equally well to just about any situation involving the operation of machines or mechanical equipment.

PACE YOURSELF !

For more detailed references on drinking and driving, on accidents and casualties, refer to the following sections in the "Guidelines" chapter of this book.

A. Pace Yourself
   Sections 5, 6
B. Preventive Thinking
   Sections 5, 7
C. Know What You Are Drinking
   Sections 4, 5, 9, 10 to 12, 14
D. Know How Your Drinking System Functions
   Sections 3, 4, 9 to 11
E. How to Be Aware of Unsafe Drinking Habits
   Section 7

4

Dining Out on the Town

Many of us begin to number among our friends and relatives those who used to be sparkling dinner companions whenever we splurged on dinner out, at some attractive restaurant, but who have lately begun to change. They have become such bores or made such fools of themselves in public that we no longer are enthusiastic about asking them to join us. Why?

For the most part, you will find that these people are in trouble and are no longer drinking safely, sensibly, or moderately. They often may start out like a rocket. But by the time the first course has arrived, they are more interested in another cocktail. And by the time they are partly through the entree they are either uncommunicative or talking without making much sense.

If *you* yourself are becoming more and more like this, you probably are not drinking safely. You may be edging into that dismal condition where the head seems to have a lead weight and you wish you could lie down for 5 minutes, just to clear the cobwebs.

On this very day, in every corner of the world, people

are drinking in one form or another in restaurants ranging from British pubs and French bistros to Mexican cantinas, German biergartens, Yankee country inns, and revolving space capsules atop city skyscrapers. Whether the toast for the occasion will be *Skoal! Salud! Nosdrovia!* or *Cheers!* diners will be enhancing their menus with alcoholic beverages to suit the circumstances.

Down through countless generations, drinking has been associated with dining, and particularly on those occasions when families and friends have gathered outside the home, free of the drudgery of cooking, setting tables, and cleaning up after the last course has been consumed. Why shouldn't it be so? Given the abundance of earth's agricultural treasures, it was inevitable that people would discover the joyful results of fermentation and distillation. After all, alcoholic beverages originate with some of the most nourishing and universal products of the land's fertile soils. Sun-drenched vineyards abound in rich varieties of grapes of every description which, when skillfully processed, yield wines that delight and surprise knowledgeable drinkers with their fragrant bouquets and delicate flavors. The flowering fruit trees and bushes that cover the globe provide the bountiful harvests of apples, peaches, cherries, berries, and other fruits that are the essence of heady cordials and other after-dinner drinks that bring meals to a pleasant and fitting conclusion. Virtual mountains of hops and barleys are brewed into the refreshing beers and ales and other malt beverages that can be offered in endless varieties and brands by public restaurants and taverns. And the great fields of corn, rye, and other such grains provide the necessary ingredients for the distillation of fine bourbons, Scotches, and other whiskeys.

With all this agricultural wealth, and with mankind's experience in transforming natural solids into potable liquids, why shouldn't we enjoy drinks that can enhance our meals and enrich our human companionship?

The answer is: We certainly should be able to do so. The occasion turns into a problem only when we let ourselves be carried away by the opportunities for overimbibing, just as we might by gorging on the varieties of food available, when we really should be watching our waistlines a bit more carefully.

When dining out, you really have to resolve beforehand just how much you care to be subjected to what in effect is a dose of anesthetic. If you are not under any personal stress, are going to be relaxed, and have no responsibilities for handling arrangements, dividing the bill fairly, or getting everyone home safely, then you can enjoy one or two moderate drinks as a positive part of dining and socializing. If, on the other hand, you have the responsibility of driving, masterminding the seating plan, and making sure no one orders outlandishly expensive items on the menu, then you had better attend to a little *preconditioning* before you set foot out the door.

A Preconditioning Plan of Action

Many people will spend hours, even days, planning a dinner party or other social event that they want to invite friends to at their home. They go to great lengths to make decisions about food, drinks, and hors d'oeuvres. They determine where and how they want to serve their guests and what they might want to do in the way of changing or enhancing the decor.

But when it comes to dining out, sometimes at considerable expense, they make no plans of any kind until the very last minute. Obviously, it is fun to decide occasionally on the spur of the moment to go out for dinner. Yet the selection of the restaurant, whether made quickly or after long planning, should be made not only with the type of food in mind but with serious consideration given to the drinking "situations" that might arise.

Is the restaurant one where the drinks are given far more attention and service than the menu? If so, avoid the place. The owner is obviously in business to make a fast dollar and well aware that the bar can produce twice as much profit as the kitchen. The restaurant may need you, but you don't need it.

If you enjoy dining out with any regularity, keep an updated list of restaurants, typical menus, prices, and the professional practices of the bartenders and barmaids. Are the latter buzzing around like honey bees, taking new drink orders before the old ones have been consumed? Then cross the establishment off your list and don't get talked into going back.

Even the best restaurants—in fact some of *the* finest— are the habitat of a specialist we could do without: the foreign-accented maître d' who gives the impression of being personally insulted if you do not order cocktails, at least two kinds of table wines with the meal, and cordials later. How do you cope with this kind of snooty majordomo who can humiliate the nondrinker with the lifting of an eyebrow? When he repeats your order of a ginger ale or spritzer, he intones the words as though they were akin to the Scarlet Letter.

The best ploy is simply to *ignore him.* He'll go away rather quickly when he sees that business at your table is not likely to be overlucrative. And never, never apologize.

Whether you are talking to the maître d', your waiter, or a barmaid, the way to order a nonalcoholic beverage or mild drink is to do so bluntly, directly, and with a firm voice. Coke, ginger ale, and tonic with a twist of lemon or fresh lime are perfectly acceptable. If you prefer not to drink, be familiar with some of the nonalcoholic beverages that have gained acceptance in drinking circles. The Virgin Mary, a Bloody Mary without vodka, is quite popular. You can order it mild or spicy, and it is served in the same way the alcoholic counterpart is. Another such drink is the Horse's Neck, which resembles a Tom Collins, has a twist of lime and some soda, but no liquor.

Strange as it may seem, waiters and waitresses do not usually blink an eye these days if a patron says, "I don't want a drink, thanks, but please bring me an iced coffee (or iced tea) when you serve the drinks to the others."

Dinner companions have even been heard to remark, "Oh, that's a good idea. I think I'll try it next time."

Innovation and ingenuity are a nondrinker's best friends.

Diet Your Drinking

Another effective preconditioning plan is to put your-self on a par with people who are dieting. Diets—whether for weight or health reasons, or both—are acceptable today everywhere in the civilized world without question. So why should it not be equally acceptable to *diet your drinking?*

The per capita consumption of alcohol in the United States alone has increased 20 percent during the past de-cade. If average Americans were eating that much more food every day, they'd be flocking to the diet centers (even more so than they already are). Hasn't anyone tumbled to the idea that most of us could well use a diet approach to our drinking habits? Such a program is really quite sim-ple, even when dining out or at a bar with friends. Here are some practical and effective tips:

1. When you go out on the town, spend more time with friends who drink little or not at all, and wean yourself away from the ones who cannot seem to engage in any social function without jazzing things up with beer, wine, or liquor. Drinks should be ordered to enhance the food, not vice versa.
2. Try starting with a nonalcoholic drink before ordering a cocktail or wine. If dinner is to last for longer than

a couple of hours, alternate your drinks with ones that contain no alcohol.

3. Practice the art of *sipping*. Beers, wines, and hard liquors (distilled spirits) originated as drinks that were to be consumed slowly and sparingly. The practice of gulping drinks is not only dangerous to your health, but crude, rude, and inconsiderate. As a rule of thumb, you should time your consumption so that one drink—no matter what kind it is—lasts at least an hour before you order a refill. Get to know your own capacity and stay within your comfortable limit, no matter how much others around you may be imbibing.

4. Downgrade your selections. If you are accustomed to drinking cocktails and straight drinks that are heavily laced with spirits, switch to highballs and mixed drinks that contain less alcohol per glass. In general, avoid drinks that mix two kinds of alcohol, such as gin and vermouth or some of those after-dinner bombs that contain a blend of cordials and whiskey or vodka. The more concentrated the alcohol is in a drink, the greater—and faster—the effect on your body. In general, it takes an hour and a half for your body to metabolize the alcohol in a standard drink. If you dilute your drink, and take longer to drink it, the impact will be less. If you intend to have wine with the meal, skip cocktails, since they mix poorly with wines and can cause distress.

5. Get acquainted with the *spritzer*. This is a light, refreshing drink combining club soda and wine. It can be made with red, white, or rosé wine and is appetizingly garnished with a wedge of lime, lemon peel, or other fruits. Since the proportion of wine to soda is 50/50, the alcohol may produce a pleasant sense of well-being without addling your brain or bringing protests from your stomach. Spritzers are becoming more and more popular, along with wine on the rocks.

6. You may want to try one of the new *dealcoholized* wines and beers that are increasingly available in the better restaurants. These are not the insipid and tasteless imitations of the past but actual beverages that have been fermented and brewed full strength and then processed so that the alcohol is removed.

7. Set a time limit whenever drinking is involved. Establish strict schedules when drinking in a restaurant or bar and either switch to a nonalcoholic beverage or get ready to go home when the deadline arrives.

8. Get rid of the unwholesome *after* syndrome. This is the obsessive urge to extend an otherwise normal social function with an extra round of drinks. There really is no great pleasure in mixing an *after*-dinner drink when you have just enjoyed a fine meal and perhaps some wine; celebrating a sporting event by having a drink *after* it is all over; or lingering at a bar to down "one for the road," which is not only a bad idea but is asking for trouble if you have any intention of driving.

Equally insidious is the *before* syndrome, which more and more restaurants seem eager to promote. This is the apparent move to attract more business during off hours by getting us into the habit of enjoying Sunday brunch. There is nothing wrong with brunch itself (other than extra calories), but the current marketing approach is to offer a "free" Bloody Mary, glass of champagne, or some imaginative alcoholic drink of the bartender's choosing. In the first place, nothing is ever free at these places. They simply cut down on the amount or quality of the food. In the second place, you really do not need to add one more drinking habit to your repertoire, especially not mid-day on a Sunday. Young people are particularly vulnerable to this kind of merchandising, and are usually too self-conscious or inexperienced to demand a nonalcoholic beverage in place of the Bloody Mary or champagne so obviously touted by the management.

One of the greatest deterrents to overindulging in drinks, especially to anyone who has ever been weight-conscious, is the number of absolutely useless calories contained in common alcoholic beverages. Here, for example, are what your caloric intakes are likely to be when polishing off a few of the more popular drinks that you might order in a restaurant or bar:

Type of Drink	Amount, Ounces	Calories
Regular beer or ale	12	150
Light beers	12	95
White wine	4	100
Red wine	4	110
Sweet wine	3	120
Cordials	2	160
90-proof bourbon	1½	120
86-proof rum	1½	110
80-proof Scotch	1½	100
80-proof vodka	1½	95
Gin martini	2	130
Whiskey highball	1½	110

The calories in alcoholic beverages are not only of no food value, but can actually destroy certain nutrients in your body, such as vitamin B and water-soluble minerals like potassium and magnesium. Beers and wines do contain a few nutrients, unlike distilled spirits, yet not enough to be of much value to your system.

Misleading Measures

A Scotch and soda is a Scotch and soda.
A martini is a martini.
A glass of red wine is a glass of red wine.
True?

No. False, because it is a fact of life that some people relate the quality of a restaurant (or bar) by the size and strength of the drinks served there. Professionals who study the effects of alcohol on people, and who make surveys of our drinking habits, generally accept *an ounce and a half* as the standard amount for a drink, no matter how it is mixed. Most people who drink regularly without experiencing drinking problems are accustomed to the 1½-ounce jigger as the proper measure for making drinks.

Yet many restaurants and bars make a habit of lacing their drinks with 2 or 3 (sometimes 4) ounces of alcohol, thus assuring themselves of a reliable coterie of "regulars" who will patronize the establishment forever—or at least until they become alcoholics and have to be carted away for treatment. The same generosity carries over into the serving of table wines, with goblets that hold 6 or 8 ounces of liquid replacing the more modest 4-ounce wine glasses.

What this adds up to is that *you have to be wary of judging your capacity on a per-glass basis!*

If you dine out regularly or occasionally meet friends at local bars, play it safe by getting to know the habits of the bartender. You cannot pace your drinking without knowing exactly how much alcohol you are consuming in any given drink and over any given period of time. (The home bartender can be just as much of a culprit, of course, as the commercial type. Many hosts in private homes seem to feel that the essence of generosity is to mix liquid time bombs for their guests, and the results often show it.)

Aren't you protected by the *shot glass,* that little 1-ounce jigger that can provide a very clear indication of how much alcohol you are getting? Only in rare instances. The shot glass, according to an experienced bartender, represents a "personal barrier" to the customer. If it is used at all within sight of a patron, the bartender usually adds a large additional splash, often with a flourish to dramatize his generosity. If you are trying to drink safely, how are you to know exactly how much alcohol you are being served?

Well, you can ask the bartender, if you are sitting at the bar. He's likely to give you an evasive answer, or at best an approximation. Forget trying to get much information from a waiter or barmaid. So you really have to judge from experience whether the restaurants you patronize give normal, above-average, or powerful drinks, using the price also as something of a guideline. Your best bet is really to stick with the beer or ale of your choice or a table wine. The restaurant's table wine is likely to be 12 percent alcohol by volume if it's white or rosé and slightly higher if it's red.

What about the size of the glass? Experiment with your own wine glasses at home, filling them to the normal level with water from a measuring cup. You'll soon be able to judge fairly accurately whether you're being served a normal 4-ounce glass or one that is 6 or 8 ounces or more. If the glass is much larger than normal, simply consider it a double order and sip accordingly.

Why should restaurants voluntarily be serving wines in larger glasses? The answer is quite simple: because customers are expecting more. It somewhat has to do with the per capita consumption of alcohol, a figure arrived at by dividing the total amount of pure alcohol consumed by the number of persons who are 16 years of age and older. In the United States, what we see is that something like 75 million people are consuming most of the alcohol. Since the "per capita" consumption is based on more than twice that figure, the actual consumption *per drinker* is actually twice as much as it appears to be.

Today the consumption of ethanol (absolute alcohol in beers, wines, and distilled spirits) is almost 3 gallons per person per year—an increase of 40 percent over the past two decades. How much is that per drinker per week? About a half gallon of wine, three-fourths of a quart of 80-proof vodka or whiskey, or 12 cans of beer.

Statistics are tricky, and meaningless unless they are carefully explained. But they can flick on a red warning light. In this case what they really mean is that the acceptability of drinking as part of the general social phenomenon is more firmly established. Drinks are not only more accessible in more places at more times, but in some cases are almost considered a necessity for people who want to dine out in proper style.

Keep pace with your own capacity and capability—not with the statistics! Learn how to avoid being pressured into drinking when you do not want to drink, especially by some waiter who has his eye on the size of the tip.

PACE YOURSELF !

For more detailed references to dining out, refer to the following sections in the "Guidelines" chapter of this book:

B. Preventive Thinking
    Sections 4, 5
C. Know What You Are Drinking
    Sections 2 to 7, 9 to 14
D. Know How Your Drinking System Functions
    Sections 6 to 8, 10, 11, 13

5

Drinking and the Business Scene

Many people are faced with working-hours situations where they are either the guest or host on an occasion where one or more types of alcoholic beverages are served. If you find yourself in such situations regularly, you are likely to encounter one additional risk in the "business" of drinking: The refreshments are *free* (or at the very least, deductible). Thus, it is easy to overindulge for two reasons: (1) Drinks are on the house, and (2), there is little guilt associated with living it up like this when, after all, you are investing your time, energy (and liver?) for the good of the business.

People who regularly find themselves in business-related situations where alcoholic beverages are commonly served sooner or later seem to have to ask themselves this question: Am I drinking too often or too much under the guise of fulfilling the responsibilities of my position?

A research study on the drinking patterns of executives documented the fact that only 13 percent were "heavy drinkers" in comparison with a national average of 12 percent. However, the category of "moderate drinkers" showed the executives with 48 percent, almost four times the national average, and with only one-fourth as many "abstainers" as the average.

Location, as might be expected, is a key factor. In Washington, D.C., for example, dining or socializing over drinks is almost a supplement to carrying on business in the office. More contacts are made, more deals consummated, more plans formulated over cocktails and highballs than in the boardroom or conference center. In large commercial centers like New York, Chicago, and Los Angeles, the importance of booze to business seems to depend as much on the nature of the operation as on the urban location. Public relations, broadcasting, advertising, journalism, and some areas of the entertainment world are particularly well-lubricated by alcohol. By contrast, bankers, architects, and accountants hardly ever touch the stuff during professional presentations and negotiations.

The contradiction here is that a person's ability to make prompt and lucid decisions is clearly affected by alcohol. It has been demonstrated that the decisions made under the influence of alcohol are often weaker and more subject to error than those made while completely sober. The typical professional or business lunch at which drinks are served may be excellent for cementing closer relationships, but it is no place to arrive at a decision or conclude a bargain. One or more participants are likely to regret the statements they made or obligations they assumed while influenced by the gentle persuasion of a dry martini or bottle of hearty burgundy.

You may not be in an industry, career, or position where this kind of relaxed decision-making is ever a factor. Yet almost every person who holds a job of any importance will become involved with occasions when drinking can be beneficial or detrimental, as the case may be. Even the much-publicized office party can turn into a disaster if participants let matters get out of hand.

Employees can sometimes be the victims of promotional schemes that encourage drinking. These are likely to be found in areas where there are large numbers of employees in a single company or industry where a kind of mass market approach can be used. Employees succumb to temptation because "everyone else is doing it," or because they have an opportunity for a "real bargain."

A division manager at one of the auto manufacturing companies in Detroit was concerned because the number of parts being rejected by inspectors on the assembly lines was increasing. Several studies of the problem quickly isolated the fact that most of the rejects were coming off assembly lines during the afternoon. Were workers getting tired? Sleepy? Lax? Not at all. They were belting down a few drinks at lunch time.

Several of the local restaurant/bars had built a competitive edge by offering a "Luncheon Special." What it consisted of was a plan whereby every patron who ordered three or more drinks at the bar was entitled to a free lunch.

Self-Evaluation

If, through necessity or choice, you find yourself involved with company luncheons, after-five business contacts, receptions, or other occasions where participants traditionally indulge in alcoholic beverages as a business activity, ask yourself the following questions:

How often do such functions occur?

How long do they last, on the average?

What percentage of the participants drink alcoholic beverages?

How many drinks are consumed by each participant, on the average?

How much do *I* drink, by comparison?

Are all of these occasions really necessary for the kind
of business I'm in?

Would I be conspicuous if I drank nonalcoholic beverages
instead of the usual drinks?

Be realistic, making a checklist if that will help you to
visualize the nature and extent of your involvement in
drinking that is related to your particular business, career,
or profession. The next important step is to evaluate
whether your drinking has increased over the past two
or three years as a result of job-related socializing. Think
not only in terms of the number of drinks you consume,
but the type and potency of the drinks. The person who
consumes two spritzers during the course of a luncheon
or two 3-ounce glasses of white wine is drinking at a much
safer level than an associate who is in the habit of downing
two large dry martinis.

In many cases when a job requires frequent lunches
with clients or customers, a deceptive progression takes
place, almost unnoticed. This is the process of *prolongation.*
The first step is the cocktail before lunch, which stretches
out the meal even before it gets started. The second is
the ordering of a bottle of table wine, which automatically
extends the dining. And the third is the habit of ordering
an after-dinner cordial, or perhaps one of several drinks
that have skyrocketed in popularity, such as Irish coffee
or Irish cream.

It's always fun to experiment—especially if the company is footing the bill. Why not try something new that's
being advertised? The experiment turns out to be pleasurable and soon becomes a habit. Safe drinking can slip insidi-
ously into *un*safe drinking through seemingly minor
changes in a person's habits.

If you find yourself slipping into some of these traps
because your job requires entertaining and socializing and

you feel uncomfortable drinking nonalcoholic beverages, then it may be time for a change. Ask yourself two questions: What are the possibilities of transferring to a different kind of position in the same company? What opportunities exist in some other organization?

The danger signals to recognize are these:

Looking forward to job-related drinking as an escape from the routine

Associating by choice with others in your organization who seem to enjoy job-related drinking

Arriving at a function early in order to have a drink before others have arrived

Stopping off at a bar for a drink before a function, excusing it on the grounds that it will put you more at ease with strangers, or business associates with whom you don't get along

Forgetting some of the points you discussed while drinking during a job-related function

Finding yourself unproductive or disinterested in your work after a business luncheon or other function at which you have consumed drinks.

The warning signal is generally the realization that *changes* are taking place in your habits and attitudes. If you have learned how to *pace* your drinking (including days when you do not drink at all), you'll recognize potential problems more quickly than if you are not continuing a regular program of self-evaluation.

Unsafe Drinking Not Related to Your Job

Quite apart from any social functions related to your position or field of work, you can use your job as a *guide-*

post to determine whether you are lapsing into any unsafe drinking habits. You do this by taking a regular "job
inventory" every few months—or whenever you feel that
problems *could* be developing. Ask yourself these seven
key questions:

1. Am I making more mistakes than normal on the job?
   If these mistakes occur regularly in the morning after
   you have enjoyed an evening of socializing and drinking, they may be attributed to your consumption of
   alcohol. There is a kind of reverse reaction here that
   bears observation. One study showed that people who
   are drinking more than they should have a history of
   making on-the-job errors on Friday afternoons. Why?
   Because their mind may be so absorbed in thinking
   about upcoming weekend parties and rounds of drinks
   that the work at hand is all but ignored. They forget
   appointments, make stupid mistakes in calculations,
   and appear distracted during meetings.
2. Is my work suffering? If you are characteristically neat
   and begin to notice a recurring sloppiness of execu-
   tion, or if you are usually well-organized but find your
   work slipping into disorganization, ask yourself why.
3. Am I arriving on the job late? The lateness is only
   one symptom. Equally significant is the fact that you
   are probably also making excuses, both to yourself
   and others, as to why you did not arrive on time.
4. Have I been absent from work more than in the past?
   If so, begin keeping a list of the days you have had
   to "call in sick," and the reasons. People whose drinking habits are getting out of hand usually cite numerous vague complaints on these occasions, such as headaches, fatigue, or "a bug that's been going around
   in my neighborhood."
5. Am I becoming edgy and critical? Feelings of insecurity
   and the impression that your co-workers are sometimes

against you are warning signs. They do not necessarily have to relate to your drinking, but you should investigate the reasons.

6. Am I becoming argumentative? If you find yourself at odds with others and inclined more to disagree with their opinions than try to understand them, ask yourself why.

7. Do I have to defend myself and my work more and more often? It may just be because you are no longer doing your job and assuming your responsibilities properly.

If you feel that you are no longer drinking safely and that a pattern exists that could lead to trouble, you should actively seek some form of counsel. If you work for a well-established company of some size, help may be close at hand. More and more organizations—from large corporations to moderate-sized companies, government agencies, associations, trade unions, and professional firms—have counseling services and programs for employees who find that alcohol is, or might become, a problem.

Why should such organizations invest time, money, and talent in programs to help individuals who are not bearing the workload the way they should? The answer is simple: Problem drinking (including outright alcoholism) costs U.S. industry alone about $20 billion annually in lost time, illnesses, accidents, and disabilities. It used to be that such programs were aimed almost exclusively at alcoholics. Fortunately, today more and more programs focus on *preventive measures*—helping people *before* they get in trouble.

One reason why managers encourage employees to seek help early is that these programs have proven to be very effective, have saved vast sums of money, and have helped to retain skilled and valued workers who might otherwise have to be fired. At General Motors, for example, one program has been so successful that it has reduced lost time by 40 percent and sickness and accident payments by as much as 50 percent and has cut disciplinary problems in half. It has been estimated that GM gets back $3.00 in savings for every $1.00 spent on its substance-abuse programs.

Many employees who become worried about their drinking are reluctant—if not afraid—to ask the company for help. "Why should I wave a red flag and point to myself as a person with problems?" is a typical reaction. "Maybe I'm on shaky ground already and this is all they'd need to hand me a pink slip and send me packing."

Experience demonstrates that such fears are unfounded. Personal problems of this nature are reviewed confidentially, almost always by the medical department of the company, or by an outside medical consultant if the organization is too small to have its own staff. Alcoholism itself is considered to be a disease, to be treated like any other prevalent illness. And medical specialists encourage people to turn to them for counsel as a preventive measure, even if they are only mildly concerned about their drinking.

Almost half the companies on the *Fortune* 500 list have programs to assist people. Most of the effort is aimed at the alcoholic, the person who must give up alcoholic beverages entirely and never drink again. More and more of these corporations, however, are encouraging people to request assistance long before their concerns about drinking become real problems.

When employees request counsel and assistance from the organizations where they work, one of the most positive aspects is that they may have an opportunity to transfer to a different position where there is less pressure and stress. If your drinking is in any way job-oriented (as in the case of having to entertain clients frequently), there is a good chance that you may have such an option.

People who have been drinking safely and moderately
for years with no problems can find themselves on the
brink of catastrophe when experiencing stressful working
conditions that did not exist earlier. You can be more
"driven to drink" by having too little to do, or too much;
by urgently needing something to relieve the boredom
of an unchallenging job, or by becoming a workaholic and
turning more and more to alcohol as a "reward" for all
the time you have donated to the job.

Worse yet, you can be brainwashed into believing that
you owe yourself a drink because you have (a) worked
hard all day long, or (b) achieved something on the job
that has earned some kind of commendation, or (c) had
a miserable round of frustrations on the job because of
circumstances beyond your control. You need only to
watch some of the beer commercials that have become
so prevalent on TV to convince yourself that you deserve
to be pampered. Advertising of this kind is particularly
crafty because there is no way you could be part of the
glorious good fellowship depicted and say to the bartender,
"Just give me a root beer, please."

This outlook, fortunately, is steadily changing as more
and more viewers realize that unsafe drinking is something
that families and individuals have to face realistically. We
are becoming more tolerant, too, in accepting the fact that
many of our friends and relatives should drink only occasionally and lightly, if at all. The transition that has taken
place on the job front is likely to serve as a model for
changes that will take place on the social front as well.

PACE YOURSELF !

For more detailed references to drinking and jobs, refer
to the following sections in the "Guidelines" chapter of
this book:

B. Preventive Thinking
   Sections 1, 2, 6
C. Know What You Are Drinking
   Sections 2, 3, 5, 9, 10, 12
D. Know How Your Drinking System Functions
   Sections 2 to 4, 6 to 8, 10, 11
E. How to Be Aware of Unsafe Drinking Habits
   Sections 2 to 4, 7
F. Reasons for Unsafe Drinking
   Sections 6 to 8
G. How to Form Safe Drinking Habits by Yourself
   Sections 1 to 3, 6
H. How, Where, and When to Seek Outside Help
   Section 12

6

The Sport and
Recreation Environments

Since alcoholic beverages have long been touted as relaxing substances, they have quite naturally come to be associated with many forms of recreation. What group of young people would go off to a beach party without taking along an adequate supply of cold six-packs? What sports fishing boat would leave the dock without drinks and setups to celebrate the hoped-for achievements of the day? What major football game could be held without its share of tailgating parties beforehand?

Nowhere does safe drinking seem to need more consideration than in those activities where people tend to throw themselves, sometimes a bit recklessly, into a pursuit that is considered to be pleasurable, often exciting, where it can be further enhanced by the consumption of beer or other alcoholic beverages. There is a tendency to let the drinking get out of hand, as it often does, for example, at a sporting event where spectators are greatly stimulated by the action. People tend to forget what they are drinking, or how much, in the excitement of the occasion.

Generally, the price paid is no more than a hangover

the next day and a resolve not to be so careless the next time. When *participation* in a sport or active form of recreation is mixed with drinking the results can be more serious. Skiing and snowmobiling are good examples. A report made on some 270 persons injured in snowmobiling accidents revealed that 75 percent of them occurred on weekends in mid- or late-afternoon or evening and that alcohol was a factor in 40 percent of the accidents. Drinking was an even greater factor—about 75 percent—in those accidents where the injuries were serious.

"The frequent combination of alcoholic beverages and high-velocity machines for relaxation and for recreational activities," said the report, "will very likely lead to further serious orthopedic injuries. The role of alcohol has become more obvious. Hopefully, preventive educational programs can reduce the hazards."

Further studies have revealed similar tales of disaster when people mix alcohol with other forms of mechanical power used for recreation, such as outboard motors, motorbikes, sea scooters, and dune buggies. Your chances of accident after you have been drinking are much higher because you are unlikely to be as familiar with their operation as you are with that of the family car. Hence, you do not have the same kind of built-in reflexes that can sometimes pull you through without catastrophe when you have overimbibed and are suddenly faced with an imminent hazard.

Safe drinking is a relative factor in the matter of sports and recreational activities. What is "safe" when you are engaged in some friendly bowling at a local alley might be highly dangerous if you are water skiing or sailing a small boat in a stiff breeze. A solid percentage of the 8000 or so drownings that occur every year can be traced to alcohol, sometimes in small amounts. Swimmers lose their inherent fear of the water and go far beyond their depth or distance. Boaters take risks they would not have otherwise or suffer death and serious injuries from falls when they lose their footing.

After two highballs or four cans of beer, average drinkers may feel great but are on the verge of losing some of the fine skills that control movement. After another drink or a can of beer, they will begin encountering some difficulties. If they are trying to catch balls or other objects, they may not only drop them but risk a split finger that may take months to heal. If they are skiing, they risk a serious fall because of deteriorating balance. If they are swimming, their poor judgment may entice them too far from shore to get back or into unmanageable currents.

Over and beyond the hazards of decreased coordination, clumsiness, and weakened judgment, the chemical changes that take place in the body during and after drinking can cause trouble. Studies of the effects of alcohol on swimmers showed a direct association between drinking and drownings or near-drownings. Not only was judgment impaired, leading to dangerous situations, but the strenuous exercise in some cases led to hypoglycemia, a condition that causes weakness and interferes with the body's temperature regulation.

Hypoglycemia is a condition that exists whenever your blood sugar level is too low to meet your body's sudden energy requirements. Familiar symptoms of this imbalance are fatigue, anxiety, irritability, and depression. One common—and very dangerous—reaction is drowsiness when driving home after a party and you are called upon to exert just a little bit more energy at a time when you normally might have been in bed. Hypoglycemia can be severe if you have had enough alcohol to cause strong chemical changes, even if you do not feel that you are at all intoxicated.

What about drinking *after* you have exercised?

If you have exerted yourself heavily, after jogging a long distance, playing several sets of tennis, cycling, or cross-country skiing, for example, your blood sugar level will be lower than normal. A beer or two is not likely to do any harm. But if you chugalug a couple of cocktails or tall alcoholic drinks, you could very well trigger a negative reaction. The result is akin to what occurs with someone who is diabetic. Your system is, in effect, shocked and you begin to feel drowsy or depressed or anxious, without ever getting any pleasurable sensation from the drink itself.

Chemical changes that take place when you are exercising strenuously after having had a few drinks can trigger other reactions that are both unpleasant and dangerous. There is reason to believe, for example, that high blood pressure can result, or that you may become subject to chronic heart palpitations and serious ailments that affect your cardiovascular system.

Athletes Who Drink

A lot of colorful prose has been written about top athletes who have competed successfully for years and yet are able to hit the bottle with great gusto in between conquests on the gridiron, tennis courts, or diamond. "They drank hard and they played hard," wrote one sportswriter in reviewing the recent past of some noted athletes. Every sport has them. Grover Cleveland Alexander drinking all night and trudging out of the bull pen to save a World Series. More than one quarterback raising hell all week and throwing the touchdown pass on Sunday. Derek Sanderson scoring hockey goals and Georgie Best scoring soccer goals and Bernard King scoring basketball goals, and all of them saying this time they were going to beat alcohol and other problems. . . .

It was not until the late 1970s that one sport, major league baseball, began doing something to help some of its star moneymakers stop drinking dangerously before their careers—and maybe their lives—were ruined. Other major sports have been slower to come to the rescue, if at all. One problem frequently cited as a cause of excessive boozing is that professional athletes are constantly on the road, often under great pressure, and living in one hotel after another where there is not much to do except head for the bar in between games.

In the long run, they ultimately prove the theory that alcohol and sports (like alcohol and driving) do not mix.

The image of the hard-playing, hard-drinking athlete has faded, particularly as the public has begun to accept alcoholism as a disease and as more and more news stories have disclosed cases of problem drinking in the sports world. Yet the image is still too much alive in the minds of some young people, largely males, who think of beer as a refreshment naturally associated with sports.

Another myth in this general area of activity is the belief that hard exercise is an effective cure for a hangover. Does it really help to get out there and jog for a couple of miles? Or plunge into a pool and swim ten laps? Or strap on a pair of cross-country skis and push through the snow for an hour? Psychologically, it may be of some help to people who really believe that they are purging themselves of the alcohol still in their bodies after overindulging the night before. But the *only* real cure is time—time to let the body's organs and tissues run through their natural actions.

If you are sports-minded, or regularly put your body through a course of stiff exercises, safe drinking is all-important. Schedule your programs in such a way that exercise and drinking do not mix—before, after, or during workouts. There is a shock effect to the system that, if fully understood by people who enjoy exercise and athletics, would truly discourage them from ever mixing the two.

You could almost parallel the alcohol/driving slogan and advise: "If you exercise, don't drink; if you drink, don't exercise."

The Exercise/Nutrition Concept of Safe Drinking

Exercise contributes to safe drinking habits in two ways. First, when properly scheduled and enjoyed, it can replace segments of daily or weekly time formerly allocated to the Happy Hour or other drinking periods that were becoming too much of a pattern. Second, exercise in itself seems to minimize the urge to have a drink (as long as you don't get in the habit of thinking you need a beer every time you get overheated!).

Nutrition contributes to safe drinking habits because the ingestion of wholesome, nourishing foods greatly reduces the urge to have a drink as a quick pick-me-up or an antidote to that tired, run-down feeling that comes from lack of healthful diets. People (especially the young) who try to exist on junk foods seem to be particularly susceptible to switching from nonalcoholic beverages to beer and alcohol when they become tired of what they are eating. These drinks replace the inner urge for sugar.

The first step is to recognize your own individuality. You may seem to fit into a certain pattern, and even be classified from the standpoint of personality and physical being as a "type." Yet you are not. Your body is a highly complex machine, whose cells and tissues and organs are marvellously related and coordinated. When one part of this intricate mechanism malfunctions, it can set up a kind of chain reaction that affects other parts. The nature and extent of that reaction is different in each one of us, often to a remarkable degree.

That is why some people can drink regularly and never have problems with alcohol, while others will be seriously affected by the same amount, or even much less. The outcome is partially—though never totally—affected by what you eat and the ways in which you exercise this complex and often demanding machine.

Ray Lyman Wilbur, a noted physician and educator, had this to say about the casual, and often careless, way many people mistreat themselves:

"Most people have little idea how to care for their bodies or how to use their brains and be well and happy. Millions of them keep themselves under the partial influence of caffeine, alcohol, nicotine, aspirin, and other drugs a good deal of the time. From childhood, they never play fair with the finest machine on earth."

Dr. Charles S. Lieber, known for his studies of alcohol, nutrition, and the liver, says that "Ethanol [alcohol] may directly alter the level of nutrient intake through its effect on appetite, displacement of food in the diet, or by virtue of its deleterious effects at almost every level of the gastrointestinal tract."

Alcohol Metabolism

The major mechanism for alcohol metabolism is in the liver, whose cells produce an enzyme that breaks down alcohol into toxic chemicals, including one called acetaldehyde. Some of the toxicological effects of alcohol are caused by the overabundance of these chemicals. There is some evidence that acetaldehyde is produced more heavily in alcoholics, drink for drink, than in social drinkers. This is one of the problems that makes it impossible for alcoholics ever to return to normal drinking.

Excessive alcohol in the body can cause disturbances in sugar, protein, and fat metabolism, leading to increased susceptibility to infection. Alcohol inhibits the liver from burning its normal fuel, which is fat, because it burns the alcohol instead. This results in accumulations of fat in the liver and in the blood (cholesterol), which may be one reason why heavy drinkers have a high incidence of coronary artery disease. Fatty liver is reversible—that is, the condition will clear up—if drinking is discontinued in time. But it takes only about four two-ounce drinks of liquor a day to risk developing a fatty liver.

If heavy drinking continues, there is a danger of hepatitis, inflamed liver cells that cause fever, jaundice, and abdominal pain. This, in turn, can lead to cirrhosis, a scarring of the liver tissues that can result in internal bleeding and is often fatal.

Alcohol is a direct cause of numerous gastrointestinal disturbances. Since it is an irritant, it often affects the lining of the stomach, resulting in gastritis, sometimes with hemorrhaging. Other alcohol-related disorders are ulcers, inflamed pancreas and bile ducts, chronic diarrhea, and a thickening of the intestinal walls. This thickening inhibits the absorption of certain nutrients, including sugars, amino acids, minerals, and vitamins. The resulting deficiencies, particularly in the B vitamins, calcium, magnesium, potassium, and iron, can lead to a wide number of medical problems. These include anemia; neurological disorders, such as numbness or weakness; amnesia, and impaired vision, caused by lack of vitamin A. Vitamin D deficiencies weaken the bone structure and make heavy drinkers more susceptible to fractures. They can also interfere with the clotting of the blood, making even simple cuts and bruises extremely dangerous because of excessive bleeding.

It has also been well established that heavy drinking can, in the long run, have a deleterious effect on the brain, interfering with such functions as the memory, coordination, and reaction. Research shows that many of the adverse effects of alcohol are reversible once patients have stopped drinking. But some portions of the brain never recover.

The Importance of Exercise

Without proper exercise, our bodies suffer because the nutrients we consume—no matter how well-balanced and how superior their quality—do not reach all of our cells, tissues, and vital organs properly. Consider the similarity to the flow of blood through the human system. No matter how "rich" our blood may be, it cannot invigorate the brain cells and the extremities of the body effectively if our circulation is poor.

Adequate exercise, in whatever form is most desirable, helps to assure a better distribution of nutrients to all parts of the body. "Exercise" is difficult to define, because it varies tremendously from one person to another. It does not have to involve miles of jogging, participation in high-energy sports, or endless routines in a gym. People who are active in their occupation or daily routine may need very little formal or planned exercise. But those who are sedentary, sitting all day at a desk or having little occasion to move about briskly, need something to "get the juices flowing."

The individuals who have the most problems with unsafe drinking are often those who are living (whether temporarily or permanently) sedentary lives. The problem is not necessarily that they have too little to do—many may be working long and hard at their chosen careers—but that their "inner environment" is stagnant. They are susceptible to a *physical* need for stimulants and body-altering substances, a substitute in effect for the nutrition that is not reaching all parts of the body in balanced proportions.

An editorial in *Journal of Studies on Alcohol* in 1982 reported that "laboratory research has indicated that improvement in fitness levels allows an individual to cope better with emotional stress. In addition, it has been suggested that regular exercise is effective in the alleviation of anxiety and depression." Getting plenty of exercise and staying fit is just one more step towards avoiding any overdependence on alcohol or, for that matter, any other substances.

A great deal of research remains to be done in this field, and many of the findings are inconclusive in studies of the relationship between exercise, nutrition, and drinking. Yet there are so many case histories of people with drinking problems who were able to counteract them by active participation in exercise programs that we have to give strong credence to the results. If you strike a good balance in the matter of exercise and nutrition and reflect on the other suggestions in this book about safe drinking, your chances of avoiding any problems with alcohol will be greatly enhanced.

PACE YOURSELF !

For more detailed references to drinking and exercise refer to the following sections in the "Guidelines" chapter of this book:
A. Pace Yourself
     Sections 2, 3
B. Preventive Thinking
     Sections 3, 4, 6
C. Know What You Are Drinking
     Sections 1, 7, 8, 13 to 15
D. Know How Your Drinking System Functions
     Sections 1 to 4, 6 to 12
E. How to Be Aware of Unsafe Drinking Habits
     Sections 5, 7

F. Reasons for Unsafe Drinking
    Sections 1, 2, 4, 5, 7
G. How to Form Safe Drinking Habits by Yourself
    Sections 1, 4, 6, 7, 9

7

Living with an Illness

Whether you spend most of your time at home, in an office, on the road, or a combination of places, the effect of drinking on your life and lifestyle will to some extent be determined by the state of your health. Despite the thousands of years that alcoholic beverages have been available to mankind, we are just beginning to learn how alcohol affects certain parts of the body.

A most important question is this: From a purely physiological standpoint, how great a consumption of alcohol is really considered to be *safe*? We can turn to one answer that has stood the test of time for well over 100 years. Back in 1862, an English physician, Francis Anstie, advised adults to "Drink no more than one and one-half ounces of alcohol each day, only with food and only in dilute form."

Anstie was speaking about pure alcohol, which in terms of today's drinks would be the equivalent of three 12-ounce bottles of beer, a half a bottle of wine, or two cocktails or mixed drinks made with 1½ ounces each of 100-proof liquor. A further specification of "Anstie's Law of Safe

Drinking," as it was officially titled, is that you cannot accumulate the daily ration and drink twice as much one day as long as you abstain the next day.

Anstie's safe limits, which have been substantiated by recent medical opinions, are based on the amount of alcohol the average human body can process in a 24-hour period without risk of damage to any vital organs. Furthermore, the drinks should be properly mixed, not taken straight, and consumed over a reasonable period of time. Three or four quick belts, even though they do not exceed the daily limit, are not encouraged.

This formula, while good for comparison, may actually be too potent for many people. In order to drink safely, you have to consider the effect of alcohol on your physical system, as well as the disruptions it can cause mentally, psychologically, and emotionally. There are two fundamental ways of looking at this: the first from the standpoint of the person who is *physically in good health,* the second from the standpoint of the person who is either temporarily ill or has some chronic condition. No matter what the nature of the condition or illness, alcohol is going to have a different, usually more serious, impact than it would on a perfectly healthy body.

The Human Body in Good Health

What happens when alcohol is swallowed in any of its various forms and begins to make its presence known within a human body in good health?

Alcohol is absorbed almost immediately—within a matter of minutes—through the mucous membranes of the mouth, stomach, and upper part of the small intestine. About 5 percent of it is excreted, unchanged, from the lungs, kidneys, and sweat glands. This discharge is pure enough so that tests of it can accurately project the total amount of alcohol in the body. The remaining 95 percent is oxidized with the aid of enzymes, or broken down, in the liver cells.

There is no way that this process of breaking down, and eventually eliminating, alcohol in the body can be speeded up. That is why you cannot sober up drunks more quickly by administering cups of black coffee, slapping them on the face, or immersing them in cold showers.

When alcohol is absorbed by the liver cells, a number of physiological actions take place that can be harmful if the ingestion continues over too long a period or in too large a quantity. These processes are many and complex. But, just by way of example, an increase in uric acid in the blood is stimulated, which if repeated over a long period of time could result in gout, a very painful inflammation of the joints. An excess of alcohol also can cause an increase in fatty acids in the blood, a condition that makes people more susceptible to such disorders as hardening of the arteries, coronary artery disease, and strokes.

We continually hear horror stories about college students who drink enormous quantities of alcohol—on a bet or during a fraternity initiation—and die. A recent, and typical, case was that of a nineteen-year-old man who chugalugged five bottles of beer and a quart of whiskey "while friends cheered him on." When he passed out, they danced around him, only to find out later that he was not unconscious, but dead. What did he die of? Acute alcohol poisoning among other things, as well as respiratory failure and the immense shock to his system.

Alcohol is a strong irritant. If you put a few drops on a wad of cotton and hold it against the inside of your mouth, you will soon notice the mucous membranes getting red. The same irritation occurs in the stomach and large intestines, or in your throat itself, the degree obviously dependent upon how much the alcohol is diluted. Alcoholic beverages in moderate amounts will have little deleterious effect on healthy tissues. If you have a sensitive stomach, however, the irritation could have unpleasant, even dangerous, results.

There has long been considerable dispute among experts over the supposedly *beneficial* effects of alcohol. An ounce or two in the evening is said to relax people with mild heart conditions, which is a reasonable assumption, as long as the drinkers don't decide that 3 or 4 ounces will logically be twice as good for their well-being. Actually, it is risky for people with heart trouble to drink at all, since alcohol can reduce the cardiac output, unless they have discussed the pros and cons with their doctor and received approval to drink on a moderate basis. Old wives' tales abound. One is that alcohol helps to "build blood." In actuality, alcohol reduces the amount of blood that can be made by the body when alcohol is present in the system.

Many people believe that a good stiff drink (or two) will help to combat infection. The premise is all wrong. Alcohol has a toxic effect on the bone marrow, which is where the white blood cells and antibodies are produced for protecting the body against various infections. Absorbed in sufficient quantities, alcohol suppresses not only the white blood cells but the formation and manufacture of gamma globulins, that portion of blood plasma that is rich in antibodies.

To put it bluntly, people who are usually healthy but begin drinking alcohol beyond the safe limits are going to be more prone to infection than they were because their internal defense mechanisms are being interfered with. Alcohol's effect on the bone marrow also reduces the production of red blood cells, causing various anemias and the production of platelets, both of which disturb the clotting mechanism.

Alcohol has been referred to as an "imitator." That is because the effect on the body of excessive drinking often resembles other disorders, such as gastritis, lesions, or liver disease. If you think of excessive drinking in terms of the harm it can do to your system, you may go a bit easier on those stiff drinks and the daily cocktail habit.

Have you ever noticed how someone who is a heavy drinker tends to look puffy? The cause, in part, is alcohol, which causes water to be retained in the body, along with the other cellular fluids. These people are actually *over*-hydrated.

If you are a normally healthy person, but starting to drink more than is safe for your particular size, weight, and physical makeup, you'll begin to get definite *warning signals*. After drinking certain types of drinks you may feel slightly nauseated, have irregular heartbeats, or find that your vision is slightly impaired. You may find that, instead of giving you the sense of well-being that formerly went with a couple of drinks, you have vague feelings that your whole system is a bit out of whack—the way you might when starting to come down with a cold.

Other warning signs are headaches while you are still drinking (long before "the morning after"); unexplained skin rashes; reddening or flushing of the skin; a burning sensation in your stomach; flurries of sneezing; and other symptoms that are often associated with various kinds of allergies. You might, in fact, be just plain allergic to alcohol, as intensely as though you were a hay fever sufferer in a field of goldenrod.

An interesting case was that of a businessman who had been perfectly healthy most of his life. For no reason at all, he began breaking out in an irritating rash at the end of the afternoon. His doctor could find nothing wrong with the man during a series of checkups and tests. The strange thing was that the problem occurred only on *weekdays*. Was the patient undergoing any new pressures or tensions on the job? No. Was there any new executive in his office who might be getting under his skin for one reason or other? No. Was there any change in the pattern of his work habits or the amount of coffee he might be drinking in the afternoon? Still negative.

Finally the doctor isolated it to lunch and something the patient had been eating. But he reached an impasse again, because the man, though he had frequent business lunches, varied his diet considerably. There was only one ingredient in all of the man's eating, drinking, and work habits: He always had a rye on the rocks before lunch. "Try giving it up," advised the doctor. The man did, and the problem with the rash disappeared. He simply was allergic to the rye in the whiskey.

The Human Body with Ailments

If you have, or are prone to, gastrointestinal disorders, alcohol will affect you more severely than in the case of people with healthy digestive systems. Irritation from alcohol that might be only a minor annoyance to a healthy man or woman can cause acute pain and distress. Repeated drinking is one of the common causes of stomach ulcers, often accompanied by serious bleeding. It is also a factor in many cases of colitis, or inflammation of the intestine, and chronic diarrhea.

Alcohol can have a marked effect on the adrenal glands, stimulating them to produce more adrenaline than normal, thus causing the blood pressure to rise. Obviously, this can be a serious situation for anyone who already has high blood pressure, and is probably already on a special, or restricted, diet.

One of the great myths about alcohol is that it can warm you up when you are cold, yet at the same time cool you off when you are hot.

Individuals with cardiovascular disease have to accept the fact that their safe drinking level is lower because it causes dilation of the blood vessels of the arms and legs and skin. This results in the false sensation that drinking warms your body, when in fact it is causing blood to be transferred from your vital organs to your extremities. The transition can be dangerous if you are exposed to the cold without adequate clothing. Uncontrollable shivering can result and in severe cases victims can suffer hypothermia, a sudden lowering of the body temperature that is sometimes fatal.

The reverse can be true in extremely hot weather, causing heat stroke to people who have been drinking too much on the beach or otherwise exposed to strong sun.

"A hot rum drink before bedtime is a great way to put you to sleep." True or false?

This is another one of those popular myths about alcohol, that it can send you on your way to a deeper, more restful night's sleep. People who have trouble getting to sleep, particularly those who suffer from insomnia, should never use alcohol as a liquid sleeping pill. Although alcohol is a depressant, it provides only a transient sedative effect, lasting about 2 hours. During the next 10 hours, while it is being fully metabolized in the body, it has the effect of irritating the nerves, causing wakefulness or restless sleep at best. The best advice for insomnia is simply to get up and use the time constructively to complete some paper work you've been putting off for days. This will usually make you drowsy in no time. Or read a good book or take a warm bath and glass of hot milk. Sooner or later you'll be dead to the world, and much better off than if you had dosed yourself with a drink.

What about the *heart*? Only a few years ago it was relatively common for doctors to suggest that certain patients have a drink occasionally in order to relax and relieve some of the stress that was bad for their hearts. One theory even had it that if you insisted on smoking you should also drink, "to dissolve the nicotine."

It is now known, unfortunately for those who believed in this kind of medication, that alcohol has adverse effects on people who suffer from certain types of heart ailments. There is, in fact, such a thing as an "alcoholic heart," which reacts badly to strong drink. Alcohol destroys a vital enzyme that is necessary for muscle contraction. When ingested in any quantity, therefore, it seriously decreases the life-sustaining functions of these muscles.

For an individual with an abnormal heart, just 2 ounces of 100-proof liquor can have marked negative results. What has been referred to as "silent coronary disease," quite common among males over the age of 40, can suddenly become loud and clear. Not only does alcohol weaken the heart's ability to contract properly, but it increases the blood triglycerides. These are fatty substances that are just as alarming as cholesterol in blocking the coronary arteries.

If you drink moderately, don't panic. When alcohol is the culprit in damage to the heart or arteries or related parts of the body, the results usually come from many years of steady, unsafe drinking. The key word here is *steady*. If you want to drink safely, make it a regular habit to enjoy a day or two each week when you abstain from alcoholic beverages of any kind. Let your system clear itself of all vestiges of alcohol on a regular basis. Let your heart pump freely for reasonable periods of time without having any kind of overload and let your blood flow freely without having to counteract any foreign substances that have suddenly been injected.

One final caution for people who are temporarily or chronically ill, under a doctor's care, yet able to drink in great moderation:

Never, ever mix alcohol of any kind with prescription drugs. The combination is more than likely to be dangerous, if not actually damaging. Taking a sleeping pill or tranquilizer with a single cocktail or highball, for example, is the equivalent of downing five or six drinks. And some combinations, in large enough doses, are lethal.

Alcohol and the Brain

Although alcohol affects those parts of the body described above, and in fact the entire human system, its most dramatic and immediate impact is upon the brain. It reaches the brain quickly after being imbibed, where it begins to depress the higher nerve centers. The inexperienced drinker is affected much more substantially, and usually faster, than the person who has become accustomed to alcoholic beverages and more or less anticipates the impact. The cerebral cortex, which is the higher part of the brain, is affected first, which changes the way the person thinks or speaks. Next in line is the sensory function, which becomes dulled so the drinker loses some of the sense of feeling. This explains why someone who is drunk can suffer cigarette burns and not realize it until later. Finally, alcohol trips up the motor function that controls the ability for movement.

Depending upon the amount of alcohol ingested, the individual loses many of the more civilized assets that have been acquired, such as consideration for other people, politeness, modesty, reserve, prudence, and anxiety or concern. Poor judgment is always one of the results of drinking too much. While this is only a temporary situation, it has been well-documented that the brain can actually suffer permanent damage in the case of chronic and excessive drinkers. Any form of drinking that disorients the brain to any marked degree just has to be labeled *unsafe.*

There are two types of cells in the brain, excitatory and inhibitory. These are what control the fine tuning of the nervous system, as well as our motor functioning and other forms of behavior. Since alcohol is a depressant chemical, it depresses the functioning of both of these types of brain cells. We know that it will alter the inhibitory cells first, which is why we often see normally shy people lose their inhibitions and assume completely different personalities after a few drinks. This is also the reason why many people think of alcohol as a stimulant rather than depressant, because it has "stimulated" unusual actions. But what really happens is that the inhibitory cells become depressed, or muted, leaving the excitatory cells to orchestrate wild and uninhibited behavior. The period of excitement and euphoria is usually short-lived. By the time the alcohol interacts with the excitatory cells, the behavior—in fact, *all* behavior, fades away as the drunk passes out cold.

The ultimate overall impact on the brain, usually felt most strongly "the morning after," is strongly depressant. People who drink chronically often say they do so in order to combat depression. The truth of the matter usually is that they are depressed because they are drinking. Unsafe drinking of this nature usually leads also to resentments, at first transitory but later becoming more and more ingrained; to imagined injustices; and to self-pity. Most of these feelings are vague and illogical, making it very difficult for self-analysis and improvement. Even psychiatrists, psychologists, and other professional counselors find themselves stumped when they try to unravel the mysteries of minds that have become disoriented because of excessive drinking. New studies are underway to determine the relationship between alcohol and the brain cells, but the results are still inconclusive.

The only real solution to the problem of excessive drinking is to abstain from all forms of alcoholic beverages—permanently.

Ethnic and Genetic Factors

In addition to the environmental factors already mentioned, the rates at which alcohol is metabolized by the body depend in part on hereditary factors. One study, for example, found that alcohol was cleared from the blood more quickly in Caucasians and Orientals than in Indians and Eskimos. These are generalizations to some extent, since additional research has shown variations among Indians, depending upon their own heritage and environment, and even on their eating habits.

The ultimate effect of heavy drinking on the body also varies significantly in different ethnic and racial groups. Although no group is immune from, say, alcohol-related cirrhosis of the liver, various segments of our society are affected to different degrees. For example, American Indians are prone to develop alcoholic cirrhosis, but American Jews are relatively spared. These differences are commonly attributed to cultural factors leading to alcoholism.

Abnormal Metabolism

This question often arises: Do the people with a tendency to alcoholism drink too much because their bodies are somehow abnormal, or do their bodies become abnormal because they drink too much?

There is increasing evidence that abnormal drinking patterns are a direct result of certain metabolic changes. There is a malfunction of the liver, for example, which causes a substance known as *acetaldehyde* to accumulate during the drinking of beverages containing alcohol. Unfortunately, acetaldehyde is a dangerous substance which irritates the cells and hampers normal cellular activities. It can also react explosively when combined with other chemical substances. The results are damage to the liver and a lower-than-normal processing of the alcohol that has been taken into the body.

Acetaldehyde's harmful effects are not confined to the liver. High levels of this chemical can inhibit the synthesis of proteins in heart muscles, increasing the risk of heart trouble. They can also cause undesirable chemical reactions in the brain, one of which may lead to alcohol addiction.

The purpose of these highly technical references is not to alarm readers into worrying whether they can be safe drinkers if they are from certain ethnic or racial groups, but to explain that there are differentials to consider. Usually the differences are slight, even inconsequential. Yet they can in some cases be part of the pattern of forming safe-drinking habits.

PACE YOURSELF !

To assess reactions to alcohol, based on your physiological, psychological, and emotional health, refer to the following sections in the "Guidelines" chapter of this book:

B. Preventive Thinking
    Sections 4, 5, 7
C. Know What You Are Drinking
    Sections 7, 8, 15
D. Know How Your Drinking System Functions
    Sections 2 to 10, 13
E. How to Be Aware of Unsafe Drinking Habits
    Sections 4, 5
F. Reasons for Unsafe Drinking
    Sections 3 to 5, 7
G. How to Form Safe Drinking Habits by Yourself
    Sections 1, 6, 8, 9
H. How, Where, and When to Seek Outside Help
    Sections 1 to 7

8

The Romantic Environment

Candlelight and wine.
Cocktails for two.
A champagne toast to the bride!
Brandy in front of an open fire.

How easy and natural it is to associate drinking with romance, for young and old alike, in many places, at many times, down through the history of mankind. Excluding those cultures where alcohol is forbidden or strongly restricted, dating, courtship, engagement, and marriage are often accompanied by some form of drinking, ranging from the minimal to the excessive. In motion pictures, on television, and in the pages of best-sellers, heroes and heroines are frequently depicted in one or more of the following situations: enjoying a candlelit dinner with wine at some elegant bistro or historic country inn; getting to know one another over cocktails on an apartment balcony or outdoor patio; sipping late-evening highballs between dances at a fashionable bar; cooling off with a frosty beer after a couple of sets of tennis.

"A loaf of bread, a jug of wine, and thou. . . ."

Sometimes the enchantment continues and the lovers who have become married still cherish the same kinds of moments, the same kinds of drinks that helped to bring them together. In other cases, alcohol—once it has accomplished its role—becomes so secondary to a couple's needs or desires that it fades out of the picture. Not infrequently, it is eliminated almost entirely from the budget for economic reasons as husband and wife devote their joint efforts to buying a home and raising a family.

But all too often alcohol asserts itself as a presumed solution to a shaky marriage, an escape from the growing problems of parenthood, a reward for sticking with a too-demanding job, or a solace for having to live in an undesirable neighborhood. Stoutly laced rum drinks may surreptitiously replace the delicate French table wine of dating days, mainly because they provide the escape or reward or solace more swiftly and decisively than the juice of the grape. Or it may become a habit to institute a late-afternoon Happy Hour to compensate for mutual boredom and lack of any satisfying hobbies or recreational programs.

This kind of trend from safe to unsafe drinking is particularly treacherous because it thrives on what seem to be logical reasons. Couples, or even whole families, can excuse the changing pattern of drinking on the grounds that it is an expedient to better—or at least less harassed—living. "Why shouldn't we drink to add a dash of romance to a life that seems to have become very drab?"

Other excuses fall conveniently in line: the increasing pressures that come from trying to keep up with the cost of living; the ironies of pursuing a family-oriented lifestyle while all around you the world seethes with hatred and crime and terrorism; the ubiquitous presence of in-laws who are always trying to impose their narrow beliefs and run your life.

Spouses and lovers should ask themselves why they

drink what and when they do, if they feel that their drinking habits are changing for the worse. If the answer starts with a defensive "because . . ." and ends with excuses, the chances are that the drinking is overstepping the limits of safety.

The Truth about Sex and Alcohol

"Candy is dandy, but liquor is quicker."

Almost everyone remembers this bit of terse verse from the past, implying that the fastest way to seduce a girl was to soften her resistance with a few drinks. This is all part of a prevalent myth that has been around for a long time that alcohol is an aphrodisiac and has great powers as a sexual stimulant. Shakespeare said it best many generations ago when one of his characters said this about alcohol:

"It provokes the desire, but it takes away the performance."

The most that alcohol can do is to remove a few inhibitions. Yet even while it is making the drinkers less resistant to the idea of a sexual encounter, it is also impairing their erotic capabilities. Upon reaching the bedroom, the person who overindulges is likely to be more inclined to sleep than to perform and thus to end up failing miserably. If the failure is repeated too often it can result in critical anxieties over one's masculinity or femininity, as the case may be. The ultimate result may be not only the loss of libido but also *psychological* impotence, which is just as alarming as its physical counterpart.

Many love affairs have come to naught and many marriages have gone sour because of one partner's tendency to turn to the bottle for stimulation prior to engaging in sex. The problem is made more acute by the depression that sets in after drinking, coupled with irritability and often hostility. This breakdown in the relationship can be excused by the offended partner once or twice perhaps, but the pattern becomes quickly ingrained so that the non-drinking partner begins to find sex distasteful and difficult, if not impossible.

Many men become impotent after even moderate amounts of alcohol and have great difficulty maintaining an erection or reaching the point of climax and ejaculation. This failure is not only unnerving at the time it occurs, but is quite likely to generate continuing apprehension and what is known in the medical field as "secondary impotence." What this means, in effect, is that during future romantic encounters the male partner may experience similar difficulty and failure, even though he has not had a drop of liquor.

Studies have shown that excessive drinking is much more likely to cause sexual problems with men than with women. The male problem lies in the transport of testosterone, the major male sex hormone that gives signals to the brain. In women, there are no acute changes in estradiol, the hormone secreted by the ovary, which is needed in pregnancy.

This discovery came as a blow to that particular type of male (of which there are too many) who has always considered alcohol to be an aphrodisiac and an aid to his skill as a seducer.

As might be expected, the difficulties and problems increase in direct proportion to the drinking. It is almost a certainty that when one partner overindulges repeatedly in a way that interferes with a couple's sex life, the other partner is likely to turn elsewhere for affection and romance, often to the point of being regularly unfaithful.

Many men express surprise and anger when this common situation occurs and they find that their wives or mistresses have strayed. Confronted with the fact that they were equally to blame, they are likely to describe their unfortunately timed drinking bouts as the result of excessive job pressure, financial stress, or family problems.

The logical advice parallels that of the admonition, "If you drink, don't drive." "If you have too much too drink, don't try to be romantic!"

From the Feminine Viewpoint

Many wives who have experienced regular romantic disapointments because of their husbands' overdrinking and failures in bed admit to an almost total lack of interest in, and sometimes an actual fear of, sexual intercourse. They cite the lack of romantic foreplay and verbal expressions of love. The husband who has had one (or a few) too many is not only drinking unsafely but unlovingly. He tends to be insensitive to the subtleties necessary for the emotional and sexual arousal of his mate, and he seldom makes any attempt at least to express in words what he cannot in actions. Romance fades away into nothingness because the relationship as lovers has largely disintegrated. In fact, if the male is too much into his cups, he is more like a child being scolded or rejected by a parent. Later, feelings of guilt and inadequacy further weaken the romantic relationship that once existed.

Although women do not threaten the emotional relationship nearly as much as men when they have overindulged in alcoholic beverages, they are vulnerable in a completely different way. More and more publicity has been given recently to studies supporting the belief that *drinking, even in moderation, is very unsafe for women who are pregnant.* You have probably seen this referred to in newspapers as the *Fetal Alcohol Syndrome* (or FAS).

Alcohol in the system follows the same course as essential nutrients and oxygen and passes readily from the maternal to the fetal circulatory system. In most cases, when the drinking is not extreme, the alcohol is rapidly metabolized and excreted by the fetus in an innocuous manner. Unfortunately, in an increasingly recognized number of cases, the effects are not that transient. Some specialists believe that *any* exposure to alcohol, though seemingly harmless, takes its toll.

Four potentially harmful effects can be observed in the newborn infants of mothers who have been drinking heavily prior to arriving at the hospital and giving birth:

1. A neurological depression, not unlike the kind that hits adults who have imbibed too heavily. This gradually subsides as the alcohol is excreted by the newborn baby.
2. Hypoglycemia, or low blood sugar. When severe, this disorder can lead to convulsions, as well as serious dehydration.
3. Alcohol withdrawal symptoms. Though this is rare, it is always a danger because of the severity of its onslaught similar to delirium tremens in an adult alcoholic who has been withdrawn from alcohol.
4. Lower birthweight. The National Council on Alcoholism urges women who are pregnant to abstain from the consumption of alcoholic beverages, since drinking as little as two drinks a day is associated with low birth weights in newborns. Unusual though this situation may be, except in the case of mothers who are alcoholics, there is evidence that unsafe drinking during the period of pregnancy can have an effect on the size and weight, as well as the health, of the newborn child. One of the main causes of this condition is the lack of proper nutrition that often occurs when women drink more than they should and then go on absurd

diets to counteract the calories they have absorbed from beer, wine, or liquor. Spontaneous abortions have been observed at consumption levels as low as two drinks per week. Fetal Alcohol Effects (FAE), less severe defects than the full-blown FAS, which appear in different combinations, are also caused by drinking in pregnancy.

There seems to be a direct relationship between the menstrual cycles and the drinking habits of some women. They may be perfectly normal drinkers during most of the month, but then have a craving for more wine or cocktails during that premenstrual period that lasts from three to seven days. In one research study, for example, it was found that two-thirds of the women in the survey group drank more heavily during this period.

Why? During this part of the cycle, women's bodies retain excessive amounts of sodium and fluids as a result of certain hormone imbalances. This condition causes anxiety, irritability, weight gain, and depression—conditions that can be partly alleviated by either tranquilizers or liquor (or, deplorably in some cases, *both*).

The Importance of Education

Since males and females react so differently to alcohol when it comes to the nature of their romantic, emotional, and sexual relationships, it is crucial that couples who are in love understand what alcohol can—and cannot—do. They also have to realize that they do not have to share the same drinking patterns in order to maintain their closeness.

Often, in fact, unsafe habits develop when a woman tries to keep pace with her mate in the matter of drinking.

She may drink more or switch from a mildly alcoholic drink, like white wine and soda, to a more powerful one, such as Scotch on the rocks. Not too many years ago, a highly popular gift item was the miniature cocktail shaker with matching glasses for two and the implication that His and Hers martinis were necessary for Total Togetherness. Brides who had never tasted gin began getting bombed; bridegrooms found the gadget a good excuse for establishing a nightly Happy Hour; and both agonized during the course of many "mornings after" that the concoction had made them argumentative and nasty.

Moral: If you're not an experienced gin drinker, eschew martinis.

People are reluctant to abandon the mistaken notion that alcoholic beverages are stimulants, especially when it comes to romance and boy-meets-girl activities. The number and popularity of singles bars attest to that attitude and outlook. There is no doubt that mild intoxication leads to a sense of well-being and confidence and greater freedom of behavior. When we drink, our guards are down. We have less sensitivity about personal relationships and are more willing to leave our inhibitions behind and get involved. For these reasons, it can truthfully be said that alcohol has been responsible for many a seduction that has taken place that otherwise would never have been successful.

In accepting this fact of life, though, it is also important to understand that people are not *stimulated* into romantic relationships by alcohol. Rather, they are *tricked* into them because their social and moral defenses are weakened. Mankind has been fooling itself, historically, about alcohol after many thousands of years of its use. So, in a social sense, we accept some of the myths as truths. The moderate use of alcohol in association with romance and sexual activity is a combination that is too ingrained in the mind to ignore.

What it all boils down to is that a little alcohol can be appropriate in many romantic situations when it is consumed at safe and reasonable levels. The heavy use of alcohol—the *unsafe* use of it—can do nothing but cause trouble. Marriage counselors and other specialists in this field estimate that from 40 to 60 percent of domestic problems between husbands and wives originate with excessive drinking on the part of one or both partners. From the standpoint of pure statistics, people who drink too much marry at about the same rate as the general population of moderate drinkers or abstainers. But they show a much higher number of broken marriages—separations and divorces—than do those groups with no history of drinking problems. The statistics apply to male and female drinkers alike. It is a curious fact, though, that many heavy drinkers continue to remarry, indicating perhaps that they continuously need this kind of close support in order to cope with the stresses and demands of life.

Looking at drinking from a more positive viewpoint, alcohol has often served a useful purpose in society by providing just enough euphoria and sense of confidence to help a romance to fruition.

Candlelight and wine? Fine.
Cocktails for two? May be taboo.

PACE YOURSELF !

For more detailed references to alcohol and its effect on your emotional and physical behavior, refer to the following sections in the "Guidelines" chapter of this book:

B. Preventive Thinking
   Sections 5, 7
C. Know What You Are Drinking
   Sections 2, 3, 5, 6, 11, 12

D. Know How Your Drinking System Functions
   Sections 3, 4, 11
E. How to Be Aware of Unsafe Drinking Habits
   Sections 2, 4
F. Reasons for Unsafe Drinking
   Sections 1, 2, 6, 8
G. How to Form Safe Drinking Habits by Yourself
   Sections 5 to 9

9

Alcohol and Youth

Despite the continuing controversy about the legal drinking age, the fact is that young people are beginning to drink at an earlier age and are consuming more drinks per capita than ever before. Teenagers, for example, who used to drink in high school on an occasional basis to be "one of the gang," are drinking more regularly. This trend has been caused in part by the ever-increasing availability of light beers and wines that do not have as much stigma attached to their use, and do not stir up as much parental objections, as distilled spirits. The consumption of fruit wines—substituted for Cokes, Pepsis, and other kinds of sodas—has escalated more than tenfold. While many of these wines contain only half the alcoholic content of regular wines, they are still about twice as strong as beer and are often guzzled as thirst-quenchers as though they were nothing more than fruit juice.

The reasons for drinking are many. Young people who are new to the job market are often influenced by older workers who have established patterns of drinking. They congregate at local bars after work as a form of relief from the pressures of the job; attend office parties; or in some cases even find that social drinking is an acceptable part of the job, such as entertaining customers. Young people who have elected to go to college face other kinds of temptations to drink. These include socializing, celebrating campus events, and all too often escaping frustrations and boredom.

Young people in their late teens and early twenties are likely to be more affected by alcohol than older adults for a variety of reasons, chief of which are the following:

1. They have not yet learned how to compensate for the changes that alcohol brings about in their physiological and psychological makeups. They do not yet realize that they may have to move a little more deliberately in order to avoid knocking over a glass or think something through a bit longer in order to reach a decision, after having had two or three drinks.

2. Their young livers are more susceptible to damage by alcohol because they are not fully mature.

3. Many are slighter and weigh less than older people and are thus affected more by the alcohol consumed when it is ingested in the bloodstream.

4. They have not yet acquired as much of a sense of judgment as older people and are likely to make errors and missteps.

5. Finally, they are likely to have more stresses and tensions, or at least be more sensitive to these pressures than older people. While some of these stresses may seem minor in retrospect—a beginning job, romantic attachments, new-found freedoms, the anticipation of traveling—they tend to be of real significance to the young and will cause a direct reaction when drinking also comes into the picture.

The Impact of Education

Since young people who are still in high school or living on a college campus are immersed in education, they are already attuned to learning and are likely to absorb information about alcohol quickly and positively when alcohol awareness curricula are made available. This assumes, naturally, that the programs are as carefully conceived and presented as any other major course of study.

One large national fraternity, Lambda Chi Alpha, serves as a constructive example. Its advisory committee on alcohol abuse recommended that a good alcohol awareness program had to increase individual and group awareness of the cost of alcohol abuse in terms of health, personal achievement, public image, human values, and fraternal respect. The committee advised that an effective alcohol abuse program had to be governed by the following principles:

An appropriate and realistic policy on the use of alcohol in all applicable situations.

An attitude that the consumption of alcohol is socially acceptable today and that this must be taken into consideration in planning educational goals.

A real and total commitment to the educational effort as a priority, with a complete understanding that the commitment must be long-range and that the immediate effect would be small.

It was clearly pointed out that, while the consumption of alcohol is acceptable within many campus social structures, all forms of behavior caused by the abuse of alcohol are undesirable. It was emphasized, too, that the risk of alcohol dependence, even among college-age drinkers, is substantial and that the topic of alcohol abuse must be dealt with and discussed seriously and not as a joke.

Most progressive schools have alcohol awareness programs that attempt to anticipate the problems and deal with them before they get out of hand. Such programs ask students the following kinds of questions, both directly and indirectly:

What are the major areas of concern among undergraduates regarding alcohol and its use?

What amounts of alcohol are consumed individually and by various student groups?

How much do you know about available resources for assistance in cases of alcohol abuse?

Are you, and others, well aware of state and local laws governing the purchase and consumption of alcohol?

Do you know the rules and regulations stipulated and enforced by the college?

How important a role does alcohol play in social and organizational events on campus, both planned and informal?

What is the general attitude of your class towards drunkenness?

What procedures have been established on campus for dealing with drunkenness?

Roughly, what percent of your classmates abstain from alcoholic beverages?

What is the general campus attitude towards students who do abstain?

Are *non*alcoholic beverages also provided at campus social functions where alcohol is served?

Is food served at functions where alcohol is made available?

Proving Out the Three-Part Approach

A college campus is an excellent real-life "laboratory" for testing and developing the three-part method of safe drinking, since it can be kept within narrow bounds and pursued in the following fairly simple manner:

1. Selecting *scenarios*. There are likely to be far fewer potential settings for drinking situations on campus than in the outside world, partly because of the limited environment to begin with and partly because of the drinking restrictions that necessarily prevail. Typical scenarios or settings would be: Formal receptions hosted by the college or faculty members; social functions at fraternities and sororities; informal beer parties; spectator gatherings at certain kinds of sports events; patronage at local bars and restaurants by students of legal drinking age; invitations to social events in the community, but outside the college.

   Most students will find that there are but two or three such settings where they are regularly exposed to alcoholic beverages, ones which they can anticipate quite easily and without any surprises. They could probably predict with 90 percent accuracy when, where, and what they will be drinking during the course of any upcoming week.

2. *Preconditioning* and programming. Since the number of on-campus or near-campus situations are limited, it is relatively easy to judge in advance what kinds of temptations are likely to lie ahead. Preconditioning becomes almost repetitive, so much so that the danger lies in becoming too indifferent and assuming that it will be easy to avoid overindulgence. "I've been through it all before," you tell yourself, then wonder the next day why on earth you ever let someone talk

you into that extra rum drink you didn't need at the end of the evening.

Knowing the situations that will arise is half the battle. But ignoring them is inexcusable.

3. *Pacing.* Once a person has become preconditioned and has accurately focused on the scenario, pacing will be much easier, though never quite as simple as the drinker might have hoped for. It is also subject to a variety of ups and downs and changes, depending upon the person's physical condition, mental state, amount of rest during the past 24 hours, and other factors.

The unfortunate image of campus parties has long been one of "beer busts" and other forms of overimbibing. The popular students were often thought of in terms of their abilities to be good party-goers, and that in turn suggested an ability to keep up with the best of them in the booze department.

Happily, that picture has gradually been changing as national fraternities and sororities have become concerned about their own images and reputations, both on campus and off. They have especially been upset by behavioral problems and the destruction of property through the misuse of alcohol, actions that have in some cases resulted in the temporary or permanent suspension of chapters by the colleges concerned.

The trend has been one of translating this concern into action, as exemplified by one fraternity that has established the long-range goal of influencing group behavior in a positive manner in regard to alcohol. The catalyst for the program is the Alcohol Awareness Task Force, which regularly publishes articles in the fraternity's newsletter to some 10,000 members, pointing out the differences between safe and unsafe drinking.

Among the steps recommended by the Task Force to counter individual and group drinking problems are:

Commitments by members to help each other whenever they suspect the existence of personal drinking problems.

The posting of *guidelines* covering the use of alcoholic beverages at all social functions.

Sponsoring parties at which no liquor at all is served, to overcome the notion that society cannot function pleasurably without alcohol.

Making it a habit to provide plenty of nonalcoholic beverages at all functions where liquor is served.

Offering food whenever alcohol is served.

Rigidly enforcing a rule of refusing drinks to any members who overimbibe, even to the extent of banning them from further parties.

Closing the bar at least an hour before the end of the party.

Providing public transportation in advance of any party where personal driving might otherwise be involved.

Posters, manuals, and pamphlets are also made available to individual campus chapters, as well as "alcohol awareness kits" for distribution to new members. Following a leadership seminar at which "Alcohol Awareness" was the theme, the Task Force offered the seminar's slide show to chapters for presentation on campus.

The overall program was so effective and so well received that it has since been adopted by other campus fraternities and sororities across the country, in whole or in part. Alcohol has since been the subject of many leadership seminars, conventions, interfraternity symposiums, and educational programs across the United States, as well as in several locations abroad.

Another long-range project to foster safe drinking on campus is the one developed by Dartmouth College in Hanover, New Hampshire, which once had a "hard-drinking image" that was increasingly disturbing to students, faculty, and alumni alike. The objective is "to raise the collective consciousness of the 4000 undergraduate students about the effects of excessive drinking."

The program incorporates an in-house policy-planning group called the Alcohol Concerns Committee; a platoon of some eighty Alcohol Peer Counselors (APCs) who assist fellow students who may be developing drinking problems; and a campus "dog and pony" show known as Outreach, which uses entertainment and drama to bring the message to the twenty-two fraternities and four sororities in Hanover. Outreach uses videotape to document student reactions, all the way from the semi-coherent mumblings of an undergraduate well into his cups to a teetotaler who grimly recounts the tragedies that have disrupted his own family because of alcoholism.

The active student participants are solidly supported by faculty members and professional counselors from outside who step in when the going gets too rough or help is needed in specific problem areas. The Dartmouth program, though initially referred to as more comprehensive than that of most American colleges, does typify the positive effort being taken by today's universities and student bodies. Such efforts are increasingly vital as states wrestle, independently and collectively, with the "drinking age" issue.

How Should a College Education Program Function?

Today, most American campuses offer some form of counsel, although much of it is of the "a little too late" variety for students who have slipped into the chronic problem stage. Still, it is an optimistic sign that college administrators have revised their attitudes significantly so that they now play more the role of counselor than disciplinarian.

The University of Michigan is a good example, in a state where the legal drinking age was raised from 18 to 21 after a rash of fatal automobile accidents. The UM program is twofold, designed (1) to teach students to drink in a responsible manner and (2) to provide effective assistance for students with drinking problems. The Alcohol Education Office established a structure that tapped four major resources:

The first was a volunteer group from Alcoholics Anonymous, whose members left little doubt in the minds of their listeners when they presented information in a realistic and decisive manner. So well were the AAs accepted that even the most suspicious and distrustful students found their drinking attitudes undergoing some dramatic changes.

The second resource was made up of staff members and undergraduate volunteers who were indoctrinated in the techniques of confrontation. Properly oriented and trained, they used well-proven methods to communicate with students who either had problems themselves or were influential in maintaining undesirable attitudes about drinking.

The third resource was a publications program that included the preparation of articles in college newsletters and periodicals, the distribution of memos to students, the use of posters and other visual aids in public places, and the compilation of opinions on alcohol from undergraduates at all levels and in all areas of activity.

The final resource was a legal one, using attorneys and law officials to clarify and present material on the laws and regulations governing misbehavior, property damage, casualties, or disturbances as a result of alcohol abuse. The implications were made clear to all undergraduates through conventional on-campus media of communication.

One important contribution made by UM has been the creation of a checklist of "Basic Confrontation Techniques" for any program of people helping people. They include the following suggestions, among others, which can be useful in almost any educational program on safe drinking:

Know the facts well, but avoid coming across like an expert, an approach that turns off many people.

Be clear and specific, discussing only the matter of unsafe drinking and avoiding other issues, even though they might need airing.

Take your time, speaking directly yet never trying to rush the subject and get it over with.

Communicate a real interest, a caring about the person involved.

Be as objective as possible about the *facts*, but don't back off from being subjective about the person if you enjoy a close relationship.

Don't be afraid to show your feelings, if they come naturally and are directed at the issue at hand, which is *safe drinking* and not moral values or character.

Talk to people when they are completely sober, and certainly not when they have had too much to drink.

Most importantly, learn how to *listen* as well as to talk.

Another campus program of immense value is known as *Bacchus*, which started at the University of Florida in Gainesville at the end of the 1970s. It has since become a national clearing house for information about drinking on campus and has local chapters at more than 50 colleges and universities in the United States. Its studies and research substantiate the belief that undergraduates must be better educated about safe drinking, if only for the statistics reported by Bacchus that some 80 percent of all college students drink alcoholic beverages.

One truth has evolved from studies of campus programs and in fact all programs that are aimed at young adults: In order to be effective, undergraduate volunteers and participants have to go through a self-examination process and understand *their own* attitudes and behavior in regard to alcohol before they can counsel or assist their peers. They have to know as precisely as possible the differences between safe and unsafe drinking for those who prefer to drink alcoholic beverages and to appreciate and accept the opinions of those who elect to abstain, for whatever reason.

Some students at a college in Connecticut discovered an interesting fact: *Not* going to a weekend party was often much more fun than attending it. They had begun to find the Saturday night blasts too boring, noisy, and repetitive. They tried organizing different types of parties, or holding them in new locations. But it was always the same. Several students solved the problem simply by staying in their own section of a dorm and holding a friendly social hour.

"We soon found out that it was nice when almost everyone else was down at the other end of the campus having a party and just a few of you were not," said one woman, who had recently transferred from another college. "The place is quiet. You can have great discussions with the people who aren't at the party and really get to know them. At a party, everything is too confused. You don't really *meet* people at all. And your conversations are all stupid, competing with the crowd, the noise level, and the number of drinks that have reduced the conversations to mere trivia."

She also had some sound advice for anyone going to a party, at any age level: "Ask yourself *why* you are going to the party. To meet people? To show off your new clothes? To kill time? To avoid being lonely? If you don't have a good reason, why go at all?"

Advertising Aimed at Youth

There is no doubt that the producers of beers, wines, and distilled spirits are spending vast sums of money to persuade more people to drink, particularly those who have just reached or are slightly above the legal drinking age. The National Council on Alcoholism in Westchester County, New York, reported that "one half of all ads in college papers are for alcohol," and that "college-oriented magazines like *National Lampoon* and *Rolling Stones* and late night television such as 'Saturday Night Live' are filled with ads for alcoholic beverages."

Does this kind of advertising have any measurable effect? One study reported that high school students (most of them under legal drinking age) are drinking twice as much as they were ten years earlier. Another study estimated that advertising increased drinking "by about ten percent."

While we can easily condemn the advertisers for over-selling a product that, when misused, can cause misery and death, we simply have to avoid using this as a crutch. It is like blaming automobile manufacturers for highway deaths because they tout their new models. The crux of the matter was, is, and always will be, *education.* Young people who are properly educated in the matter of safe drinking and who learn how to consume alcoholic beverages moderately and sensibly are not going to be that much swayed by advertising. Certainly, they may switch from one brand to another, or from one type of drink to another. But the very act of switching can often be more beneficial than harmful—if they know what they are doing and have taken their lessons to heart.

Those Other Drugs

People tend to think about booze on the one hand and "drugs" on the other, not classifying alcohol in the same category as marijuana or barbiturates. Alcohol is every bit as much a drug as these, combining several of the effects of the others. This book will not explore the various other drugs that are most commonplace, except to point out that *combining* alcohol with one or more of them is a very dangerous practice.

We live in a society, unfortunately, where prescribing drugs to ease pain and make us comfortable is far too common a practice. After a time, we become dependent upon them, whether we are in any great discomfort or not. If we begin to think of a prescription drug in the same breath as an aspirin tablet, we overlook the potency of what we are ingesting and begin to think nothing of having a drink at the same time, or soon after. That is where the trouble starts.

Drugs have what is known as "synergistic effect." One sedative pill taken at the same time as a second pill of the same kind results in a simple addition of the effects. But when combined with another drug of equal potency (such as alcohol) the effect is *multiplied.* It's the difference between adding five plus five on the one hand and multiplying five times five on the other. This creates a dangerous situation, with a strong effect on the body.

Always remember: Alcohol and other drugs (even the most commonplace and acceptable ones) *simply do not mix.*

PACE YOURSELF !

For some references to alcohol as it relates to young people, see the following sections in the "Guidelines" chapter of this book:

A. Pace Yourself
   Sections 1 to 6
B. Preventive Thinking
   Sections 3, 5 to 7
C. Know What You Are Drinking
   Sections 1 to 5, 9 to 11, 14
D. Know How Your Drinking System Functions
   Sections 1, 3 to 5, 9 to 12
F. Reasons for Unsafe Drinking
   Sections 1, 2, 8

10

Other Settings Where Alcohol Plays a Role

You find yourself on a jet, anticipating a pleasant flight to some vacation destination that will require a few hours in the air. The plane has hardly become airborne when one of the stewardesses concludes her friendly greeting to the passengers by announcing that drinks will shortly be served to any who desire them. The implication is that you should start relishing in mind just what kind of relaxing, heartwarming potion you would like to (*a*) shorten the trip, (*b*) overcome your fears that the starboard engine sounds as though a bearing were loose, or (*c*) transform you into a jolly conversationalist so you can get along swimmingly with the strangers who are your cabin mates.

Sure enough, two or three young ladies, who don't look much over the legal drinking age themselves, soon come by with an astonishingly varied collection of drinks in tiny bottles that look anything but lethal. Here is your big opportunity to sample something you've never tried before. After all, you don't want to seem stuffy and ask for a soft drink or tea!

The only trouble with this scenario is that too many

people who find themselves airborne frequently because of business trips begin to make a habit of sampling the wares, compliments of the XYZ Corporation that is paying their travel expenses anyway.

If you travel frequently by jet, the best way to drink safely is to follow the pattern you are accustomed to at home, depending upon the time of day and the length of time involved in flight. Avoid the temptation to accept drinks at odd hours of the day, just because you happen to be en route during times when you would never consider drinking while at home. Remember, too, that alcohol affects people more at high altitudes, even in a pressurized cabin.

Friendly though they may be, airline personnel are instructed and trained never to push drinks of any kind on passengers. They will serve fruit juices, coffee, tea, and sodas just as cordially as alcoholic beverages.

Vacation travel to faraway places opens up all kinds of opportunities for imbibing, along with plenty of common and perfectly logical excuses, of which the following are just a few:

We're on a *pleasure* trip, aren't we, so why not live it up a little bit? We may never get back here again.

It's costing us a bundle to come all the way down here to the Caribbean for ten days. We might as well enjoy one of the best bargains in the islands—ten varieties of rums that don't cost any more per bottle than a six-pack of local beer back home.

The hotel is having a complimentary cocktail party for new arrivals. We'd better drink up our share, since everything else from then on is coming out of pocket.

You just can't visit the night spots without sampling some of the native liqueurs. They're made from coconut milk and breadfruit.

You don't have to be a spoilsport, of course, and refuse to experiment with things that are new and different, and all part of the travel experience. If you drink, you might want to take the opportunity to indulge yourself a bit. But find out first what you are getting into. Many so-called "native" drinks are no more authentic than plastic souvenirs, heavy in calories and loaded with enough alcohol to keep a brass lamp burning for the duration of your stay. Furthermore, if you overindulge in drinks that are real bombs you may end up with stomach trouble that will make the rest of the trip more of a misery than a vacation. Just because a drink is laced with alcohol doesn't mean that it's sanitary.

If you are a moderate drinker and intend to drink while traveling abroad, learn something about the customs and attitudes towards alcohol that you're likely to encounter in the countries you visit. In Italy, for example, the habits and outlooks are natural and relaxed. When Italians go to restaurants, most members of the family are likely to enjoy wine. Drinking is a quite natural part of dining and, as a result, Italians are brought up not only knowing about alcohol, but respecting it and living comfortably with it. In Italy, where drunkenness is socially unacceptable, you can almost be assured of safe drinking if you follow the local customs regarding the use and abuse of the grape.

If you go to France—which would seem comparable to Italy in the matter of wine drinking—be more cautious. The French tend to use alcohol for almost every function where two or more people are gathered together. Alcohol is used much more often than in Italy for purposes other than a sociable meal, whether it be getting over a disappointment, celebrating a success, or getting in a more expansive mood at a social affair. And many of the French beverages—such as the brandies, which are prevalent all over the country—are far stronger than beer or table wines.

Knowing *what* you are drinking and *why* you are drinking can be all-important.

Differences in Ethnic Drinking Habits

An article recently in *Alcoholism,* a journal for professionals in this field, discussed the attitudes and habits of various ethnic groups towards drinking and alcohol abuse. Selecting the Irish and the Jews in America as examples, the editorial reported that "the beverages chosen, companions, setting, and the degree of intoxication typically differ." The illustration pointed out that "Irish more often drink at public bars, Jews in private parties. The Irish are more likely to drink beer than are the Jews, and the Jews are more likely than the Irish to drink wine. Jews more often drink with both men and women present, the Irish with members of their own sex. The Irish tend to drink more than the Jews."

If you were to attend social events within a number of such ethnic groups, you would find that each has a distinct way of drinking and that there are clear differences in the rate and consumption of alcohol between them. Not only does the ethnic background influence the pattern, but there are even more pronounced differences if you divide the groups along other lines—such as males only, or subgroups belonging to certain social strata or economic classes.

It makes a considerable difference, too, whether you are drinking with a predominantly younger or older generation, for the outlooks and customs can vary markedly from one age group to the next within the same ethnic culture.

A study by the National Opinion Research Center revealed an interesting truth about safe drinking: Ethnic groups that have been drinking safely and moderately for hundreds—perhaps thousands—of years do not avoid alcohol. In one group sampled, only 5 percent were abstainers "and the vast majority drink fairly regularly."

We would like to be able to report that some kind of "safe-drinking formula" emerged from these studies, which could be passed along to the reader. But the *reasons why* certain groups have such a low percentage of problem drinkers remain obscure. "Whatever protects certain ethnic groups," reported the study, "apparently protects them specifically from alcohol abuse, not from substances or problems more generally."

One revelation, however, was that there is such a thing as a "cultural recipe" that dictates which substances are proper to use and in what amounts and to what purpose. A familiar, though oversimplified, example would be that of two social groups within the same community. One drinks to get high and the other to enhance sociability. If you were to attend a party hosted by the first group, you might be considered an outcast if you abstained or elected to stick with drinks that were mild. Obviously, if you were enjoying social intercourse with members of the second group, you would be under no pressure to drink anything except what you wanted. It is apparent that one's safe-drinking habits can be jeopardized or strengthened depending upon the particular scenario and situation involved.

Oriental Attitudes and Practices

In the orient, or among oriental cultures elsewhere, drinking customs and attitudes are much different than in the west, often associated with religious events or family celebrations in which foreigners are seldom invited to participate. The Chinese drink moderately in public and at the kinds of social events that might be attended by westerners. They tend to sip drinks slowly and politely. So if you find yourself in the company of Chinese at a gathering, at home or abroad, you are likely to be among safe drinkers. Any party hosted by Chinese will have food in abundance, for that is as much a part of the festivities as are the drinks. Consider yourself fortunate if you are able to sip drinks without looking too self-conscious, for the Chinese often feel that westerners drink too rapidly and with too little appreciation of what they are consuming.

Many other oriental cultures follow these same patterns and traditions, although in Japan they are becoming more westernized and less conservative. Overindulgence has become more commonplace, partly because the younger generation has accepted the cocktail party as an entertainment feature that is foreign to its elders. In Tokyo and other large cities, you will find plenty of bars and restaurants and night spots that dispense the same kinds of drinks you would find in American cities. If you sample Japanese drinks, be wary of some of the beers, which can be quite strong, and the national drink, sake, a fermented liquor that looks innocuous and is often served hot in rice porcelain cups. Yellowish in color and with a taste not unlike sherry, it contains about 16 percent or more alcohol by volume and can deliver quite a kick.

The best rule of thumb when drinking abroad is either to stick with those alcoholic beverages that are familiar to you or, when they are not readily available, to drink unfamiliar drinks slowly and cautiously. Drinking patterns can vary widely within the same country, as well as within cultures that otherwise have similarities. In the United Kingdom, for example, there are great differences in the drinks, as well as the habits, in England, Northern Ireland, Scotland, and Wales.

Customs Governing Drinking on the Job

Since more and more people in all kinds of careers are being transferred to other countries as foreign representatives of their home organizations, one question has to be faced head on: What are the customs relating to business entertaining?

There are about as many answers as there are countries.

In some cities, like Moscow, drinking is almost a part of the ritual of doing business. In others, like the cities of the Arab world, alcohol is strictly taboo, even when entertaining a business associate in one's own home. The best rule of thumb is to avoid alcoholic beverages entirely until you can become familiar with local customs. After that, if drinks seem to be in order on certain occasions, exercise caution.

Drinking Attitudes and Social Customs in the Soviet Union

Our understanding of Russian behavior is complicated by the multiplicity of occasions that are associated with drinking. Alcohol appears at virtually every pleasurable event, as well as during every situation where there is likely to be pain, unpleasantness, or stress. Russians drink when they meet each other and when they part; to quiet their hunger and to stimulate their appetite; to get warm when it is cold and to cool off when it is hot; to wake up when they are drowsy and to fall asleep when they are wakeful. A large amount of drinking occurs at most family-oriented events. For example, prolonged group drinking bouts are not uncommon at Russian weddings. Although drunkenness has been condemned by the government and the press alike, the Soviet culture by its very nature encourages heavy drinking.

It is almost expected that guests arriving at a formal

dinner will find individual bottles of vodka at each place, as though it were ordinary water. The Russian citizen who does not drink socially—particularly the male—often finds himself in embarrassing situations. He risks offending his companions and being classed as something less than a man if he refuses to drink, and even more so if he does not join in the many toasts that are expected during social occasions.

Drinking (fortunately for women) tends to be a male activity in the Soviet Union, starting at an early age. It is common practice for a father to give a glass of wine to his four- or five-year-old son to "get him used to it, so he can drink like a man." When the boy reaches his teens, he often becomes accustomed to drinking with the veterans in his factory every time pay day comes round. In fact, he is usually initiated into this practice by being coerced into spending his entire first paycheck on alcohol.

Westerners who travel in Russia are somewhat protected by the fact that most of them are on tours and not directly the guests of Russian individuals. If, however, you are likely to be in a situation where you are socially involved, be aware that Russians do not drink like Americans or other westerners, mixing and diluting their alcohol. The Russian drinks straight vodka or whiskey, usually quickly and on an empty stomach. They are seldom condemned for overindulgence in public when the drinking occurs on a special occasion, on holidays, or to celebrate some personal achievement. If you try to emulate them, you are likely to be in trouble.

Drinking and Driving Abroad

"If you drink, don't drive; if you drive, don't drink."

This advice has become increasingly pertinent in the United States, where state and local police have stepped up programs to catch and punish offenders. Abroad, especially in Europe, offenders risk far greater penalties in many countries. Even in Russia, punishment is severe, though fairly uncommon because of the scarcity of private cars.

If you drive a rented car abroad, leave it in the garage if you intend to have so much as a single cocktail. In Denmark, for example, you can be jailed and fined for getting behind the wheel after having imbibed no more than a few glasses of table wine. The practice there, when going to a party, is to have one member of the group serve as the driver and abstain from drinking, or to hire a car or a taxi.

This is not a bad idea for safe drinkers anywhere on earth at any time when alcoholic beverages are being served.

Travels to Other Countries

If you are a moderate drinker and like to drink when traveling abroad, it is a good idea to find out in advance what the public attitudes are towards alcoholic beverages, drinking by males and females separately or in companionship, and of course overindulging. It will save you possible embarrassment, as well as help you to enjoy your visit. Here, for example, are some thumbnail descriptions of attitudes and customs in several countries not previously mentioned:

Sweden: Drunks in public places are arrested and held until they are completely sober. They are fined, with increasingly larger fines for each conviction, and duly reported to public boards of temperance. Driving while intoxicated is a serious offense.

England: People who drink too much in public can be imprisoned overnight and have to face the local magistrate the next day. There is very little in British law to guide these magistrates in dealing with inebriates, although fines are generally nominal. There are no special sobering-up facilities in jails or elsewhere. The British tend to look on overindulgence as "bad behavior," frowned on by people with any sense and upbringing.

West Germany: Drunkenness, unless behind the wheel of a vehicle, is not a punishable offense in West Germany. However, in some areas there are sobering-up stations, which are compulsory and for which there is a small charge. Driving while intoxicated (DWI) is a serious, punishable offense, with stiff fines and usually loss of one's driving license. Visitors to Germany should not attempt to imitate the beer-drinking practices of some of the locals, who seem able to imbibe stein after stein and still stay on their feet.

Switzerland: Since this country was one of the first in the world to accept the concept of alcoholism as a disease, the Swiss tend to be sympathetic towards individuals who overindulge, on the premise that they may be alcoholics. Nevertheless, they take prompt action in the case of people who become drunk in public and offer a number of sobering-up services, with extended care if necessary.

Canada: Attitudes towards drinking tend to be quite parallel to those in the United States. However, the outlooks and laws vary considerably from province to province and community to community.

Latin America: Brazil may be somewhat typical in that the police and other officials generally tend to let sleeping drunks lie where they drop, as long as they are not blocking traffic or infringing on anyone's rights. Bartenders, however, are held specially responsible if they are caught serving drinks to people who have already had too much. During special occasions, like the Mardi Gras, all rules are totally relaxed. Argentina and Uruguay have so few problems with public inebriation that it is left up to the friends of individuals who have overindulged to take care of them in whatever manner they choose.

In the matter of drinking, the best advice really stems from that old saying, "When in Rome . . ."

PACE YOURSELF !

For more detailed references to drinking in unfamiliar environments, refer to the following sections in the "Guidelines" chapter of this book:

C. Know What You Are Drinking
     Sections 1 to 7, 9 to 12, 14, 15

11

Guidelines

The preceding chapters have covered common locations and familiar situations with which most readers can readily identify and which often are accompanied by the drinking of one or more kinds of alcoholic beverages. References at the end of each chapter have been to specific sections of this chapter of the book, designed to help readers evaluate their own drinking habits and attitudes more clearly and accurately.

Those earlier chapters covered the commonly *identifiable circumstances* in which drinking patterns are established and continue. The eight sections in this chapter contain the kinds of information that are less easily visualized, yet vital to the development of a workable safe-drinking program.

The questions have been selected by the authors as those that are most pertinent to each area of concern covered in the eight sections.

The answers are by Nicholas Pace, M.D., based on his long experience as a counselor in the field of alcohol and drinking.

(A) PACE YOURSELF

1. *Q.* The book has mentioned "scenarios" and "settings" as very important factors in your system of developing and maintaining *safe-drinking habits.* What do you mean by these terms?

    A. I look at them much the way a doctor might who is trying to determine the reasons behind a patient's stubborn allergy. We look at the locations and situations to determine where the patient may have problems that stem from unsafe drinking. We obviously rule out places where he has *not* been, though such locations might be significant in diagnosing other patients. These are the *scenarios.* In the case of drinking, for one person they might be cocktail parties, the family dinner table, cookouts and picnics; for someone else, receptions, business luncheons, and posh city restaurants.

    Q. Say that I have a mental image of four such settings, then what?

    A. The next step is to determine *what* you drink and approximately how *much* on these occasions. If the amounts and your reactions to drinking are negligible then you are apparently drinking safely and will have no problems as long as your drinking does not increase. To put it another way, if drinking does not interfere with your health, job, or interpersonal relationsips, then it is not a problem.

2. *Q.* What if I'm concerned that I may be drinking too much on certain occasions—do I have problems?

    A. Yes, possibly, if drinking has become a concern. You have to ask yourself whether your consumption of alcohol seems to be too heavy in all of

these situations or in just one. If you are fortunate enough to find that the latter is true, you're
best alternative is to avoid that one scenario altogether—if you can. If your drinking appears to
be unsafe across the board, then you have to
plan and undertake immediate corrective measures.

Q.   Such as?

A.   Alternating nonalcoholic drinks with the alcoholic beverages, "dietizing" your drinking, or
"stepping down" the type of drinks you select—
to name a few countermeasures. We'll cover
these later, in the section on Preventive Thinking. The drinker whose consumption is occasionally too heavy in just one situation should plan
ahead to take corrective action.

3. *Q.*   How can I drink safely in this kind of situation
if the very act of drinking "relaxes" my judgment
so I don't respond the way I would when stone-
cold sober?

A.   By *preconditioning* yourself so that your judgment
while in full command of your faculties carries
over into situations when you are drinking.
It's almost like a reflex action that has been programmed into your brain—like not touching
a hot burner on the kitchen range.

Q.   What kind of preconditioning are you talking
about that would accomplish this?

A.   *Timing* your consumption of alcohol for one
thing, so you don't overload your system. Delaying the first drink is a good way to start.

4. *Q.*   Sometimes hosts and hostesses *push* drinks on
their guests. What if I feel self-conscious or uncomfortable trying to turn down or postpone
that first drink?

A.   Watch how this is handled by people you know

who are light drinkers—safe drinkers. In fact, whenever possible, try to attend social affairs with friends who are sensible drinkers and avoid the ones who imbibe too much too quickly.

5. *Q.* One of the problems I have is that I don't seem to have much control over situations that develop at a party. How can I avoid typical problems?

A. You probably haven't anticipated these "situations" and thus tend to fall victim to circumstances. One of the most common, of course, is the problem of transportation—ending up departing in a car whose driver has had too much to drink because you couldn't devise an acceptable excuse to avoid being an unwilling passenger. This is a very typical situation which should be included with the various personal scenarios you will already have envisioned. And you will handle the situation much better when you have planned in advance how to precondition yourself, even though a few drinks may have temporarily weakened your sense of judgment.

The best slogan in the world is "If you drive, don't drink; if you drink, don't drive."

6. *Q.* What should I do if someone makes a drink that is too strong?

A. You can always ask to have a little water added. But if you feel self-conscious about that, just take the drink and later set it down unnoticed. If you are at an affair where you can make your own drinks, simply remake it to your taste. Most pushy hosts don't wait to see whether the guests actually drink what they concoct, so you can unload the "bomb" when they are not looking.

Q. Suppose you don't have much choice? What if you get stuck with the drink and then are seated next to the host or hostess, engaged in conversation so that it would be awkward to try to remake or get rid of the drink?

A. Learn how to *sip.* An important stratagem in this regard is to get in the habit of occasionally setting your glass down, rather than holding it constantly in a "guzzle" position.

Q. What are some of the alternative tricks that you mentioned earlier?

A. We'll get to those in the section on Preventive Thinking.

(B) PREVENTIVE THINKING

1. *Q.* What is a good way to program yourself, in effect, into this safe-drinking pattern of yours?

  A. Pacing yourself by starting with tall, nonalcoholic beverages. This not only reduces your tendency to gulp the very first drink, but postpones the introduction of alcohol into your system. Then, after you've consumed your first drink of beer, wine, or distilled spirits, return to the nonalcoholic beverage. First one, then the other . . .

2. *Q.* You suggested a "step-down" technique. What is that?

  A. Picture the drinks you consume most often, whether wine, beer, whiskey, or other. Then change your habits by stepping down to something less potent. For example, switch to highballs from cocktails; or from a wine with a 12 percent alcohol content to one with only 9 or 10 percent.

3. *Q.* Suppose I drink beer? Do you consider that an alcoholic beverage? And aren't all beers pretty much the same?

    A.   Beer is definitely an alcoholic beverage, and all beers are by no means the same. A 16-ounce can of regular beer contains as much alcohol as a highball made with an ounce and a half of liquor. There are some beers—referred to as "near beers"—that are lower in alcoholic content. And there are a few others that have had the alcohol removed, down to less than 1 percent.

4. *Q.* Is there such a thing as an "alcohol diet"?

    A.   Why not? I recommend that people "dietize" their drinking, just as they would the solid food they consume. Bear in mind that many drinks have substantial calorie counts. Some drinks, like cocktails that are heavy in sugar or rum, may have 300 or more calories in a single small glass. Others, like a white wine spritzer, have 50 or less.

        Of course, if you alternate drinks with ones that have no alcohol at all and are low in calories, you are better off all around.

5. *Q.* Do most people really know the nature of the drinks they consume from time to time?

    A.   Absolutely not. I am always astonished at how *little* people really know about drinks they say are familiar to them. Ninety-five out of a hundred people could not tell you the actual potency of the cocktails, highballs, wine, or beer they drink regularly. Very few drinkers know such a simple fact as the meaning of the term "proof." And even fewer could describe how alcohol affects the body and brain. Mishandling alcohol can be just as lethal as mishandling a gun or a car. Yet no sensible person would use guns or drive cars without some basic information about their safety requirements.

6. *Q.* To get back to *pacing,* is that a component of "preventive thinking"?

   A. Yes. All my steps to safe drinking really relate to *pacing.* When I talk to young people I often like to compare that to jogging. Runners may cover short distances at relatively fast speeds, long distances at much slower speeds. In either case, they may be going straightaway on flat terrain, or up and down a hilly winding course. They may also adjust their pace in accordance with what they did yesterday, or are going to do tomorrow. In order to get from here to there sensibly, healthfully, and beneficially, they have to pace themselves by judging the various factors well in advance.

   It is much easier for experienced joggers to plan ahead than to find themselves in difficulty en route. Equally important, individuals have to think in terms of their own conditions and capabilities—not push themselves beyond their limits in order to keep up with a group that is out of their class.

   Pacing yourself in the matter of drinking is the best way I know to enjoy alcoholic beverages in moderation and avoid the problems of overindulgence.

7. *Q.* Will switching drinks keep you from getting drunk?

   A. Only if you switch to nonalcoholic ones. It isn't the "drink" that causes inebriation and hangovers; it's the amount of alcohol that counts.

(C) KNOW WHAT YOU ARE DRINKING

1. *Q.* What is *alcohol?*

   A. It is a colorless liquid that is usually produced

through the fermentation of fruit juices, sugars, grains, or starches in the presence of yeast enzymes. It mixes quickly and easily with water and is also referred to, chemically, as *ethanol,* or *ethyl alcohol.* This is the agent in all alcoholic beverages, despite their differences in body, color, or formal classification, that causes intoxication.

2. *Q.* What are the classifications of alcoholic beverages?

A. There are five basic types: Beers, table wines, dessert wines, liqueurs, and distilled spirits. There are a number of specialty beverages that are combinations of two or more of these classifications. But they tend to be fads that come and go and are relatively insignificant in the pattern of drinking. Their relative potency is catalogued by actual alcoholic content, as well as by proof.

3. *Q.* What is "proof"?

A. In distilled spirits, such as whiskey, vodka, gin, or rum, the percentage of alcohol is historically expressed in degrees of proof, rather than as a percentage. This form of measure derived from an old English custom of providing proof that an alcoholic drink was potent by mixing it with gunpowder and trying to ignite it. If the drink contained 57 percent alcohol by volume it could be ignited. Proof is approximately double the percentage of pure alcohol. A 100-proof whiskey, for example, is 50 percent pure alcohol. (To ignite gunpowder the British had to use a whiskey that really packed a wallop—114 proof.)

4. *Q.* What are some of the drinks classified as "beers"?

A. The beer we are most familiar with is *lager,* with an alcohol content of 4 to 5 percent. *Ale* is the name given to certain kinds of pale beers made with more hops than beer and has about the same alcohol content. *Bock beer* is a specialty beer that is heavier and darker, originating at the bottom of the barrel, and usually sold in the spring. It tends to be on the stronger side, about 6 percent alcohol. Porter is a strong, dark ale, brewed with the addition of roasted malt to give flavor and color. Stout, which is even darker and maltier, may attain an alcoholic content of 6 to 7 percent. Malt liquor, a much more recent blend, is also at the strong end of the scale.

5. *Q.* What are the characteristics of different kinds of wines, particularly from the standpoint of knowing their potency and drinking them safely?

    A. In terms of safe drinking, volume for volume, wines run a close second to beers. The natural wines, which are not fortified or given additives, are low in ethanol and the "higher alcohols" that make drinks more potent. The ethanol (or alcohol) content of every bottle is given directly as a percentage by volume, and so indicated on the label. Red, white, and rosé table wines contain about 12 percent alcohol. Champagne has about the same alcoholic content, but is often thought to be stronger because the carbonation (whether natural or injected) literally propels the ethanol into the drinker's bloodstream faster and produces a more concentrated impact on the system.

6. *Q.* We hear a lot about sherry as a mild drink, often preferred by little old ladies or people with digestive problems. Is this a "safe" drink?

    A. That depends on the amounts and speed of consumption. Dessert and aperitif wines contain appreciably higher concentrations of alcohol than table wines. Sherry, for example, which is both an aperitif and an after-dinner drink, contains 20 percent alcohol by volume. Port, muscatel, and some of the others in this category range between 19 and 20 percent. The vermouths (both sweet and dry) are a little over 17 percent. As a matter of comparison, a 3-ounce glass of sherry equals a highball made with an ounce and a half of 80-proof bourbon. The deceptive thing here is that someone who thinks of sherry as a "sissy" drink, or for those "little old ladies," might down all 3 ounces before a more cautious drinker would sip half of a whiskey highball.

7. *Q.* Do wines have any food value?

A. In one sense, they do. Ordinary table wines are really quite complex, containing many dozens of organic compounds, including vitamins, minerals, sugars, acids, ketones, and aldehydes. Depending upon the nature of the soil in which the grapes were cultivated, wines yield minute, but measurable, quantities of aluminum, boron, calcium, copper, iodine, iron, magnesium, potassium, sodium, and other inorganic compounds.

Q. What about vitamin C, which is so prevalent in grapes and other fruits from which wines are made?

A. Vitamin C is destroyed during the fermentation process. However, wines do contain appreciable amounts of other vitamins, such as thiamine, riboflavin, and nicotinic acid, as well as nitrogen compounds, organic acids, and peptides. Dessert wines have larger concentrations of the B vitamins than the table wines.

8. *Q.* Articles have been written claiming that certain

types of wines have medicinal value. Is this true?

A. In a marginal way. Three or four ounces of a good, natural table wine is thought by many experts to be an effective appetizer and an aid to digestion if consumed slowly just prior to or at the beginning of a meal. Some specialists believe that wine is useful, in moderation, in reducing blood cholesterol levels because of substances called polyphenols that are present, particularly in red wines. It has also been demonstrated that certain pigments that pass from grape skins into the wines can have inhibitory action against some pathogenic bacteria like *salmonella* and *staphylococcus.*

9. *Q.* What are the safety factors to consider in regard to various kinds of whiskey?

 A. The most important consideration is the *proof* of the whiskey being consumed. The normal range is from 80 proof for an inexpensive blend of rye to 100 proof for a full-bodied Scotch— or from 40 to 50 percent alcohol. "Distilled spirits," which include whiskeys, contain small quantities of other types of alcohol besides ethanol. These are referred to as "higher alcohols," and usually increase slightly as a whiskey ages. Bourbon, rye, corn, and Irish whiskeys contain the greatest proportions of higher alcohols, while Scotch is very low and Canadian whiskey is the lowest.

10. *Q.* Where do gins and vodkas fit into the picture, as far as safe drinking is concerned?

 A. Like whiskeys and other distilled spirits, the first consideration is the proof, to determine the potency of the beverage being prepared, whether it is to be served straight, as a cocktail, or mixed with various kinds of carbonated beverages. The trend has been away from the 100-proof gins and vodkas to those that are only 80 proof. One reason is *cost,* because the price usually goes down in direct proportion to the proof. Gins and vodkas tend to have smaller proportions of the higher alcohols than whiskeys. However, unlike beers and wines, they are very low in solids and thus are more rapidly absorbed into the bloodstream than either of those beverages or whiskey.

11.   *Q.*   Rums seem to have slipped in popularity recently. Is that because they are too heavy or too likely to cause bad hangovers?

    A.   Over the years, all drinks rise and fall in popularity. The trend today is towards the lighter drinks, the ones that are lower in calories as well as in alcoholic content. That may be one reason why rums are less in demand in many locations. The Jamaican and New England blends contain high amounts of other alcohols, although the Puerto Rican rums have virtually nothing but ethanol. Rums may have gotten a bad name because some of the more expensive brands ranged as high as 150 proof, meaning that they contained 75 percent alcohol! Also, there is a tendency to use rum as a basis for very fancy, "tourist-type" cocktails, like mai-tais, which are garnished with colorful tropical fruits and sometimes much more liquor than the drinker suspects.

       Though not necessarily popular these days in drinks, many people like the taste of rum, which is why it is used so often to flavor desserts.

12.   *Q.*   Are liqueurs and brandies to be avoided by anyone who wants to drink safely?

A. Very few people really know how to drink liqueurs, and even fewer can handle brandies.
They are, for the most part, very high in alcoholic
content, including an above-average share of
higher alcohols. This is particularly true of co-
gnac. Brandy is actually a strong alcoholic spirit
that has been distilled from wine. Usually it ma-
tures in casks for at least four years. Liqueurs
are strong beverages made from nearly neutral
spirits that are flavored with herbs, fruits, or
other mixtures, and usually sweetened. The processes and ingredients are often strict secrets,
guarded by the producer. The percentage of alcohol by volume is printed on the labels of
liqueurs, ranging from 27 percent for crème
de cacao to 30 percent for anisette, curaçao, and
kümmel, 40 percent for Benedictine, cointreau,
kirsch, ouzo, and Scotch liqueur, and as high as
55 percent for Chartreuse. Ounce for ounce,
liqueurs of 40 percent and over are equal to distilled spirits in potency. Since they are usually
consumed "straight up" (without any mixer) or
"on the rocks" (mixed only with ice), they can
carry quite a wallop if not sipped very, very
gently.

13. *Q.* Do distilled spirits have any food value?

A. Distilled spirits—whiskeys, gins, vodkas, rums,
and other liquors—have virtually no nutritional
value. They are devoid of vitamins and negligible
in organic or inorganic compounds. All they contribute to drinkers are naked calories. Distilled
spirits imply two distinct types of risk. The first
is that their alcoholic content is absorbed much
more rapidly into the system than is true with
beers and wines. The second is that the low nutri-

tional value of distilled spirits can be detrimental to people who drink heavily and eat improperly. The results can be more frequent infections, vitamin deficiency, and even anemia, as well as general poor health. In addition, the rapid absorption of spirits through the upper gastrointestinal tract irritates the tissues during the process of being absorbed.

14. *Q.* Why is the alcoholic content of distilled spirits absorbed more quickly than with beers and wines, and what actually takes place in the body?

A. Alcohol is unique in several ways. It is totally soluble in water and thus is absorbed directly from your stomach into your bloodstream by simple diffusion. Beer and wine contain other ingredients that slow down or inhibit this diffusion. When you drink bourbon or gin or vodka, particularly in cocktails, you are imbibing a larger proportion of alcohol to other substances. Hence, the action is more abrupt. Wines work more slowly, the exception being champagnes and other sparkling wines. Carbonation increases the speed with which the stomach empties and hence quickens the impact of the alcohol on the brain. Club soda and other carbonated beverages can also speed up the process when mixed with whiskey, gin, or other distilled spirits—so keep that in mind when deciding what kinds of mixers to select.

15. *Q.* Are the *contents* of alcoholic beverages listed on labels, the way they are with food products?

A. Very seldom. In some cases, as is true with many liqueurs, the ingredients are closely guarded secrets that are known to only a few people in the producing organization itself and are never revealed on labels, or elsewhere. Critics of the liquor industry often complain that "Your right to know, as a consumer, stops at the liquor label." In the past, some ingredients in alcoholic beverages have proved to be unsafe, if not actually toxic. One example was cobalt sulfate, which was added to certain beers to insure a foamy head. A number of deaths occurred before this chemical substance was barred. There is no cause for alarm today, since the industry polices its products and procedures carefully. Still, it would prevent widespread allergy reactions and some drinking problems if consumers could read liquor labels and know exactly what they were putting into their stomachs.

(D) KNOW HOW YOUR DRINKING SYSTEM FUNCTIONS

1. *Q.* Since we read so much about drinking these days in newspapers, magazines and books, and see so many programs about alcohol on TV, aren't we pretty thoroughly "educated" about alcohol?

   A. Quite the contrary. About 99 percent of everything we read or view is focused on problem drinking and alcoholism. We need to pay a great deal more attention to *safe-drinking* habits and outlooks for people who are not in the problem category. The situation is comparable to a discussion of dieting and nutrition. If all the information centered on obesity or malnutrition, people who are of normal weight or slightly over would never learn the proper values of foods and how to eat properly and healthfully.

2. *Q.* Is it true that if you gradually increase your consumption of alcohol you will have to drink more and more in order to feel the same effects?

A. Yes. The need for progressively higher doses of alcohol to induce greater effects is known as *tolerance.* Although the exact mechanism is unknown, it is probably caused by adaptation of the nervous system to high levels of alcohol in the blood. This condition tends to mute or dull the reaction to alcohol. So, instead of feeling a little glow after two drinks, you need three or four to get the same effect. That is why a person can easily slip into unsafe drinking habits, especially if they judge their drinking by the way alcohol makes them feel. Increased tolerance is a danger signal that something is changing in your drinking system.

3. *Q.* If I drink a cocktail with, say, an ounce and a half of alcohol, what actually happens to that alcohol in my body?

A. Like other drinks, alcohol first reaches the stomach. People are advised to eat something when drinking, since the food slows the second step, absorption through the walls of the digestive tract into the blood and tissues. Most of the alcohol passes down into the small intestine, from which it is rapidly absorbed and distributed throughout the body. The swifter the flow, the higher the accumulation of alcohol in the blood and the greater the impact on your system. Some beverages contain food substances that, in themselves, slow this process of absorption. Beer is a good example. Or any drinks that have been mixed heavily with juices, milk, cream, or other liquids that in themselves have substantial food value.

4. *Q.* Is the alcohol distributed throughout the body?

   A. More or less. But its greatest impact is felt in the place it hits first—the brain. Alcohol acts directly on the brain to disrupt its ability to function properly. Bear in mind that alcohol is actually an anesthetic. When involving small amounts of alcohol, this dysfunction is minor, often stimulating the "glow" that normal drinkers feel when they have their first drink. But after a certain amount reaches the brain, judgment becomes impaired. The next step is the increasing lack of muscle coordination. That is why people who are drunk will weave, stumble, and have trouble keeping their balance. Ultimately, if too much alcohol reaches the brain, the drinker will pass out, becoming just as unconscious as though physically struck on the head.

5. *Q.* Is passing out the same as "blacking out"?

   A. No, although the two conditions can exist at the same time. Since alcohol affects the brain, it obviously can have a considerable impact on the memory of a person who has been drinking too much. The resultant blackout is a loss of memory about everything that transpired after the drinker had consumed a certain amount of alcohol. The next day, the victim of a blackout will remember things that happened up to a point, but be very foggy about what happened thereafter. This blackout phenomenon should be a red flag to anyone who feels that drinking is reaching unsafe proportions.

6. *Q.* Is alcohol injurious to the stomach?

   A. Generally not in small amounts, when consumed by people who have no serious stomach disorders to begin with. In fact, some alcoholic beverages, such as might be consumed in one or two small drinks, increase the flow of juices in the stomach and act as appetizers. Remember, though, that alcohol *can* be an irritant to the stomach lining and that this increased flow of gastric juices might be harmful to people with ulcers or other stomach ailments, especially if there is no food in the stomach at the time. Regular heavy drinking can cause chronic inflammation of the lining of the stomach, leading to severe gastritis. One of the reasons why people sometimes vomit after having consumed too much alcohol too quickly is that the severe irritation caused by the beverage acts as a defense mechanism and prevents the alcohol from getting into the bloodstream.

7. *Q.* How seriously are the kidneys affected by alcoholic beverages?

   A. Despite notions to the contrary, alcohol is not always damaging to the kidneys, except in severe cases. The obvious immediate effect is the increase in urinary action. This comes about because of the direct stimulus, not on the kidneys, but on the pituitary gland, which is a tiny extension of the lower part of the brain that controls the production of urine. When alcohol impedes the activity of this gland, the kidneys form more urine.

8. *Q.* We read about the connection between alcoholism and liver diseases. For the ordinary drinker, who may occasionally imbibe too much, are beer, wine, and liquor likely to cause any liver problems?

   A. Not if the liver is healthy to begin with. In severe intoxication, the liver may become swollen and tender, and in acute cases, this could lead to hepatitis. However, bear in mind that alcohol is greatly diluted by the time it reaches the liver and has little direct effect on that organ unless the exposure is continuous. The consumption of large amounts of alcohol can cause secondary problems, though. For example, it might cause the sugar that is normally stored in the liver to move out into the bloodstream. The same is true of vitamin A and other substances stored in the liver. In general, the liver helps to eliminate the alcohol from the system.

9. *Q.* How is alcohol eliminated from the body?

  A. About 5 percent of the alcohol a person drinks is excreted unchanged from the lungs, kidneys, and sweat glands. The remaining 95 percent is changed into carbon dioxide and water through oxidation or metabolism. Most of the alcohol is oxidized in the liver, through a series of steps that change it into an acid and then into carbon dioxide or water. That is one reason why the health of the liver is so important. Other types of food go through this process, providing the body with heat and energy. But alcohol is oxidized slowly and at a fixed rate—so precise, in fact, that the time can be determined by a formula. The formula is based on a number of factors, including the weight of the person, the amount of alcohol consumed, and the speed with which drinks were imbibed. That is why chemical tests can determine whether the driver of a vehicle is legally "under the influence," despite protests that he only had "a few beers" or had not been drinking for several hours before being stopped by the police.

10. *Q.* If the process of absorbing and eliminating alco-

hol is so exact, why do some people seem to be able to hold their liquor better than others?

A. People who have "hollow legs" should heed this condition as a warning signal that they are drinking too much. The reason they seem less affected by alcohol than moderate drinkers is that their metabolic tolerance to alcohol increases as they habitually become accustomed to consuming more alcohol. They have to drink four or five cocktails to get the same level of euphoria that they formerly achieved with two or three. Even though they may not get "high" and show the effects, they may still have their judgment and motor abilities impaired. If you restrict your intake of alcoholic beverages and drink sensibly, it is unlikely that you will build up this kind of undesirable metabolic intolerance.

11. Q. Can your body speed up the elimination of alcohol if you drink black coffee, take a cold shower, go jogging in the fresh air for a few blocks, or chew vitamin tablets?

A. Not in the slightest. These are among the most prevalent myths about alcohol. Psychologically, you may feel that such measures are helpful. But, physiologically, there is no change. Nothing but *time* can be effective in eliminating the alcohol from the system. The only thing black coffee will do is to keep a drunk awake when everybody around him was hoping he'd go to sleep and stop being obnoxious.

12. Q. Why and how does alcohol dry out the body, so that people with hangovers always have a tremendous thirst?

A. The notion that alcohol "dries out" the body is only partly correct. What actually takes place is not the elimination of water in the body, but a shift in its location. After people drink too much, water is transferred from inside the cells of their bodies to locations outside. The water thus becomes extra cellular and the cells become drier.

13. *Q.*   Are some people *allergic* to alcohol?

   A.   Very much so. It always amazes me that people who have allergies and are concerned about what they eat and where they live pay no attention at all to what they drink. Almost everyone knows that alcoholic beverages are made from such solid foods as fruits, berries, grains, and a few other ingredients that are often barred from restricted diets for people with asthma, hay fever, or other allergenic ailments. They are fooled by the clarity and seeming "purity" of the liquid flowing from the clean, simple lines of the bottle. One of the clearest of all beverages, Holland gin, for example, is loaded with traces of ingredients that might be suspect for someone with an allergy. These include juniper berries, barley malt, bitter almonds, caraway seeds, anise, cassia bark, fennel, orange peel, licorice, and even a derivative of turpentine. Many cordials, some of which were formulated during the middle ages as medicinal syrups, contain complex mixtures of herbs and spices whose exact nature has been guarded for generations.

   Even beers can be a real source of trouble, since they contain herbs, barleys and other cereals, bitter hops, and yeasts, as well as artificial flavorings and preservatives. Unlike nonalcoholic beverages and foods, beers, wines, and spirits do not have to announce their contents on their labels.

(E) HOW TO BE AWARE OF UNSAFE DRINKING HABITS

1. *Q.* In general, how can you distinguish a normal social drinker from one who has drinking problems or who may be an outright alcoholic?

   A. Looking at the subject objectively is not always easy, since heavy, compulsive drinkers are often clever at camouflaging the extent and nature of their drinking. People who enjoy alcoholic beverages in a sensible manner usually display healthy attitudes towards drinking. They exhibit a take-it-or-leave-it attitude towards drinks, seldom feel that a party is a bust if alcoholic beverages are not served, and never try to force a drink on others. By comparison, people who have developed a need for alcohol not only want to be able to have it at a social gathering but also want others to drink with them, rather than getting by with soft drinks or juices.

2. *Q.* What are the early warning signs that a person is becoming dependent upon alcohol?

   A. You may be slipping into unsafe drinking habits if you:

   Find yourself thinking about drinking more frequently than in the past . . .

   Begin wanting a drink long before some social event occurs . . .

   Sneak a drink before a party gets under way at your home or that of a friend . . .

   Stay at a party or other event longer than you had intended in order to keep drinking . . .

   Switch from the drinks you normally select to ones that are more potent . . .

Gulp your drinks instead of sipping them casually.

3. *Q.* I find that if I have had a tough day I can relax better by fixing a drink. Is that bad?

   A. Not necessarily, as long as it doesn't become a habit. Those TV beer commercials go overboard when they keep emphasizing that people who work hard *deserve* a beer when they come off the job. But they are not entirely off-base in equating a drink with healthful relaxation. The problems develop when people

   Drink more whenever the pressure gets heavy and they cannot unwind any other way . . .

   Drink every time they have a major disappointment or a squabble . . .

   Drink because they have no other kind of safety valve, such as hobbies or exercise . . .

   Drink as an escape from the rigors of their lives rather than as a form of relaxation.

4. *Q.* What is alcoholism?

   A. A chronic disease that progresses from an early, physiological susceptibility into an addiction characterized by changes in tolerance, physiological dependency, and—most important—*loss of control* over drinking.

   People are considered alcoholics if drinking interferes with one or more components of their lives, whether their social life, jobs, health, or interpersonal relationships.

   Q. Do we know what causes alcoholism?

   A. Alcoholism is a very complex disease, involving a combination of physiological, psychological, emotional, genetic, and sociological factors. Alcoholism strikes in many forms and with varying degrees of intensity, just like cancer, heart ailments, and any other major disease. Patients who suffer from alcoholism are sick, not weak, sinful, or immoral.

Q. What are the most acute signs of alcoholism, as contrasted to occasional overindulgence or problem drinking?

A. The signs are definite and clear-cut. Ask yourself the following:

Am I able to handle more liquor than I used to without showing it?

Have I noticed that I cannot drink as much as I once did without feeling uncomfortable?

Do I wake up on the "morning after" and have a blank memory about last night?

Do I often feel guilty about my drinking?

Do I get irritated if my family or friends make any comments about my drinking?

Do I have "reasons" for my heavier drinking?

When completely sober, do I regret some of the things I did or said while drinking?

Is drinking making my home life unhappy?

Is drinking interfering with my work?

Has my drinking caused financial problems?

Do I ever drink alone?

Do I have a chip on my shoulder about people and think friends are turning against me?

Do I sometimes have the shakes in the morning and find that a quick drink helps?

Have I been hospitalized because of drinking?

Do I keep a private supply of liquor so that I won't be caught without a drink?

If your answer is "yes" to even one question, then you are losing control of your drinking.

5. *Q.* What are some of the *physical* signs of alcoholism that you notice with people who drink too much?

   A. The physiological clues are many and have to be evaluated independently, then in relationship to each other. You see, some of these symptoms could suggest diseases that are in no way connected with drinking. The following symptoms are among the most commonplace:

   Pale or yellowish skin, perhaps with red blotches

   Hand tremors and quivers

   Inflamed, enlarged, or soft liver

   Poor sense of balance

   Problems with reflexes

   Enlarged heart

   Elevated blood pressure

   Anemia, or other problems with the blood

   Nausea or diarrhea

   Face flushed or pudgy

   Neuritis

6. *Q.* According to newspaper articles, social drinking in the United States has increased quite substantially. Does this mean that fewer people are drinking safely these days and that there are probably more alcoholics than ever before?

   A. Statistics can be misleading. There is evidence that a larger percentage of the population is drinking than in the past. Of great concern is the fact that some 20 percent of the drinkers are consuming 80 percent of the annual purchases of alcoholic beverages, averaging some 25 gallons per year. What we have to worry about particularly are the borderline groups, the people who *could* become problem drinkers if they are not properly educated about alcohol and if they avoid taking stock of themselves.

As for alcoholics, no one is really sure whether the ranks are increasing or remaining at a proportionate level. We do know that more and more alcoholics are admitting to, and facing, the drinking problem today than in the past.

7. *Q.* In brief, what advice do you have for everyone who would like to be aware of unsafe drinking habits?

A. Keep your consumption levels low; avoid patterns of periodic drinking; lean towards beverages that are lower in alcoholic content; always have something to eat when you drink; learn how to sip drinks and avoid gulping; plan on days when you have no alcoholic beverages at all and get out of the habit of drinking every day. In other words, pace yourself so that you are always in control of your thoughts and your actions. The instant you find that you are slipping and letting the drinks take control, then it is time to admit that your drinking is *unsafe* and do something about it.

A good slogan to keep in mind: "If you *need* a drink to be social, you are not a social drinker."

(F) REASONS FOR UNSAFE DRINKING

1. *Q.* Going back to the roots, why do so many people even start to drink alcoholic beverages to begin with?

A. "Peer pressures" are cited very often as one of the reasons why people start to drink, especially when they are in their early or middle teens. But you cannot rule out the fact that many people start their eventual drinking habits simply because they *like* the taste of a beverage. They are given a glass of wine at dinner or a cold beer on a hot day and, while they may not enjoy the taste initially, they begin to acquire a liking for it. Also, of course, they find it pleasing that a certain mellowness is induced by the drink.

Q. People also acquire a taste—sometimes on the first sip—for certain soft drinks. But that doesn't mean they then drink them to excess. Why should alcoholic beverages be any different?

A. For one thing, wine and beer become associated fairly quickly in a young person's mind with conviviality and pleasurable companionship, and oftentimes with romance or with exciting events. It all adds up to a direct association with good times and the impression—though often unconscious—that certain alcoholic beverages are the key ingredient.

2. *Q.* You mentioned "peer pressure." How significant a factor is that in drinking, and more importantly in unsafe drinking?

A. We think of the term largely in connection with young people in high school or even junior high, who are pressured into drinking against their will by friends and classmates and who have not been properly educated about alcohol and its effect on the mind and body. But this same peer pressure is a strong factor in adult patterns of drinking and is one of the important reasons why many people slip into unsafe drinking habits.

Q. Can you give a characteristic example?

A. A common one that comes to mind is this. You go to a football game with a group of friends, all more or less your own age. They make a party out of it, arriving an hour early so they can "tailgate," passing out food and drinks. You're not in the habit of drinking liquor at noon, but you go along with the idea. By the time the game begins, you have consumed more drinks than intended and feel cheerfully high, ready to go into the stadium and root for the home team. After a few more football games, you are a confirmed tailgater. The fact that you have a few drinks is not as important as the fact that you have established a pattern for drinking in midday, which finds further fulfillment in brunches or sociable lunches where a Bloody Mary or whiskey sour now replaces the tea or coffee you used to get along with on such occasions. In effect, peer pressure changed your attitudes and habits.

3. *Q.* Another reason I have heard for alcohol abuse is "solution drinking." What is that?

A. Solution drinking is, unfortunately, commonplace. This is the result of subtle, invidious reasoning that equates drinking with problem solving. One familiar example is that of the people who drink more than they should at cocktail parties because they then feel more popular and less sensitive about being left out of the action. Other examples are taking a few belts to overcome shyness or timidity or to smother depression, loneliness, or grief. Unfortunately, alcohol taken under these circumstances only magnifies the inner problems in the end.

4. *Q.* Do many people drink to alleviate physical distress?

   A. As far as we know, the proportions of people who do are not large. Taking a stiff drink once in awhile to counteract a toothache or muscular agony is not a serious cause of unsafe drinking. However, we are concerned about the numbers of people who use alcohol as an antidote for insomnia or chronic nervousness. Ironically, although alcohol may initially be effective, its influence is short-lived and it may not only aggravate existing conditions but also actually cause new ones.

5. *Q.* Alcohol, then, is a poor tranquilizer?

   A. Yes, even though chemically it is related to ether and in large doses can achieve the same results, causing unconsciousness and even death. But alcohol takes some 12 hours to metabolize completely. During the first 2 hours, it does act as a sedative. For the next 10 hours, however, it is actually an *irritant.* Alcohol is also a depressant. Within a short time—after the first couple of hours following the last drink—the person who has consumed too much begins to feel depressed, physically as well as mentally. Quite a few people use alcohol as a substitute for other drugs, such as tranquilizers. Their reasoning is that they may consume a little too much alcohol but "it's better than being on a prescription drug." See how easy it is to rationalize drinking when you compare it with an alternative that is even worse!

6. *Q.* Historically, writers, artists, and others who are creative and imaginative have tended to abuse alcohol. Is there any validity to the reasoning that alcohol stimulates one's creative abilities?

   A. Many people with creative lifestyles have equated their drinking with the enhancement of their talents. Some of the most successful writers and artists have, indeed, been alcoholics. But the unanswered question is: How much *better* might they have been if they had never hit the bottle? We are talking about such a small percentage of the population that the message can never be clear to most of us. Still, many people do excuse their unsafe drinking habits on the grounds that they need alcohol to stimulate their imaginations or set free the inhibitions that are stifling their talents.

7. *Q.* You hear the statement all the time, "I'm exhausted, I need a drink!" Are you treading on treacherous ground if you drink when you are fatigued, and especially if you use that as an excuse for opening the bottle?

   A. There is nothing wrong with having a drink when you are "exhausted," as long as you are healthfully tired and more physically so than mentally. Two cautions are in order: the first is not to use exhaustion as a regular or periodic reason for drinking. The second is not to finish more than one or two drinks under these conditions, and preferably ones that are low in alcohol content.

8. *Q.* What are some of the other common "reasons" for unsafe drinking?

   A. We have already mentioned quite a few, but you might bear the following in mind as well:

   Fear of being criticized or considered sanctimonious for ordering a soft drink instead of an alcoholic one.

   Trying to appear more sophisticated or worldly wise when in the company of strangers.

Using alcohol as an antidote to nagging or criti-
cism from a relative or spouse, or as a means
of getting along better with a hostile in-law.
Adding sparkle to a boring situation.

The list is almost endless. People who drink
too much regularly or periodically could (if anyone could persuade them to do it) make a specific
checklist of the reasons they give, whether aloud
to others or inwardly to themselves.

A good buzz word to keep in mind is HALT.
Never take a drink when you are:

> **H**ungry
> **A**ngry
> **L**onely
> **T**roubled

(G)   HOW TO FORM SAFE DRINKING HABITS BY YOURSELF

1. *Q.* What is the most difficult initial hurdle for people
who have admitted to themselves that they may
no longer be drinking safely and who want to
establish safe habits?

   A. Probably the *time* factor. When people eliminate
drinking situations from their lives or shorten
the periods when they drink at social events, they
sometimes have the sensation that they are creating vacuums that have to be filled with some
other stimulant or activity. The mellowing effects
of the alcohol may be missed, along with the
lessening (real or imagined) of the action that
used to take place. It is very important that these
vacuums be filled with something else of real
substance. If people decide, for example, to cut

out a daily cocktail hour before dinner, then they need some kind of constructive action to replace the drinking. Some of the well-proven substitutes are hobbies, sports, voluntary jobs, and part-time work. Schedules need to be changed, too, so there is no deadly gap between the dinner and the end of the workday. Avoid activities that are too similar to the old pattern, such as continuing the Happy Hour, but consuming soft drinks instead of alcoholic ones. It is too easy to start having a stronger beverage "just now and then" and gradually slipping right back into the old habits.

2. *Q.* Suppose that you are locked into a pattern that is very difficult to change, where it is difficult to avoid an ongoing occasion that is attended by your spouse, relatives, or close friends, such as a weekly club meeting?

A. Your situation is tougher. One solution is not to drink at all. Remember that every time you *do not* take a drink you build up your resistance to taking a drink in the future. Alcoholics have to accept the fact that they can never have a drink again. Since one drink leads to another, they do not have a chance. Normal drinkers who are slipping into unsafe habits can apply this strategy to those occasions that seem to involve the greatest temptations to overindulge. Use the A.A. principle of "one day at a time." Tell yourself: This is a day when I don't drink.

3. *Q.* Suppose that I have eliminated those occasions that were trouble spots in the past, but do get involved in other situations where I intend to drink, how do I make sure that I drink *safely?*

A. Make it a practice to start off with a beverage

that is tall and nonalcoholic. Sip it slowly, not as though you have to down it quickly in order to "qualify" for your first alcoholic drink. When you are finally ready for something stronger, select a beverage that is low in alcohol content. Sip it slowly also and buffer it with whatever food may be offered. If you are going to attend an event where liquor is served, but no food, eat something before you leave the house. Lastly, determine ahead of time at what point in the proceedings you will bid your adieu. Stick to your plan and don't stay for "one last drink" even at the urging of your host and other guests.

4. *Q.* How do I cope with the situation when I really want to cut down on my drinking or change my habits, but a lot of my friends are drinkers and tend to overdo it on occasion?

A. You have two alternatives, neither of which is an easy one: The first is to shift your activities gradually so that you are with them less often during drinking occasions. That does not mean that you have to avoid them, but simply be with them when alcohol is not a factor. On the tennis courts, for example. Or participating in community services. Or enrolling in courses and workshops. The second alternative is to give up drinking entirely or drink only mild beverages like wine spritzers, and let your friends know clearly that you are cutting back or abstaining altogether. If the friendships are solid, your wishes will be respected. If the relationships are weak, then it won't matter in the long run anyway.

5. *Q.* One of the problems of cutting down on my drinking is that I keep thinking about some of the good times when a few of us really "tied

one on" and celebrated some event that was important to all of us. How do you get around this?

A. Balance those thoughts off by thinking about some of the good times you had in which alcoholic beverages were not a factor. Liquor certainly is not always the ingredient that makes a party successful or that brings good friends together on congenial occasions. But don't be too eager to make comparisons. The best way is to let things take their course as naturally as possible, not overthinking the situation and not letting your life get too complicated. "Keep it simple!" is one of the best pieces of advice ever developed by alcoholics who have successfully become abstainers. You don't have to be an alcoholic to put your lifestyle in sharper focus.

6. *Q.* Does it make sense to learn more about alcohol itself, what it is and how it affects you physically, mentally, and emotionally?

A. Yes. Studies bear this out, that people who *know* more about alcohol are less likely to fall under its spell. It's a parallel to the old military strategy of getting to know the enemy as intimately as possible. Strictly speaking, we should not consider alcohol an "enemy" of mankind. It's simply another one of the hundreds of drugs that may be put to good use or to bad use, depending upon a wide range of factors that include circumstances, experience, judgment, and common sense. Yet it is certainly very true that you will be more likely to drink moderately, or more safely, if you have a clear picture of what happens to ethanol from the moment the glass touches your lips to the time it is absorbed into the bloodstream and until much later when the alcohol content has been totally oxidized and eliminated from the body.

7. *Q.* Is it important for people to know why they want to drink less dangerously, or should they just plunge into one program or another?

   A. Yes, because *why* you decide to limit your drinking will determine *how* you are going to accomplish that objective. Are your reasons physiological? Psychological? Emotional? Or sociological? Make up checklists for each category, listing the main problem areas. If you get depressed easily or have feelings of loneliness, you definitely should not drink much late in the evenings because the depressant effects of alcohol will hit you at the worst possible time, early the next morning. If you are going to face a lot of pressure on the job on a particular day, avoid alcoholic beverages the day before. If you have palpitations of the heart or find that your blood pressure is getting higher than normal, switch to drinks that have low alcoholic content, and pace yourself as you drink. If you have social problems, such as feelings that friends have turned against you or are too critical, ask yourself whether your recent patterns of drinking have had anything to do with these changes in attitude.

   In other words, the reasons *why* you need to revise your drinking habits will provide the clues as to *how much* you should cut back, and in *what ways*.

8. *Q.* What are the pros and cons of seeking professional advice, for people who want to form safe-drinking habits?

A. You *have to* take the first step, even if it's nothing more than agreeing to seek help, at the urging of a relative or friend. Thus, if your first step can be a constructive effort on your own behalf, so much the better. If you can start cutting back and evaluating your problems, you will be way ahead of the game, even though later you might have to have help to stay on target. You will have a more respectful image of yourself, will get to know yourself more realistically, and will benefit by the learning process.

The disadvantages of doing it by yourself are that you do run more risk of failure and in certain cases you could aggravate a small problem into a large one. Also, it is very hard to sit back and be objective about yourself and determine whether you are making real progress or just fooling yourself.

9. *Q.* What other suggestions do you have about forming safe-drinking habits by yourself?

   A. Here's a short checklist to add to the others:

Make sure you are eating properly and have the right kind of nutrition, to help counteract any desire you may have for alcohol.

See your doctor for a general checkup, to make sure there is no physical problem.

Line up plenty of substitute activities, to keep you busy and avoid getting restless.

Postpone making major changes in your life or assuming new responsibilities.

Avoid socializing with friends who are heavy drinkers. Seek out friends who drink little, or abstain.

Start a physical exercise program.

If relevant, step up your sexual activity.

Avoid sleeping pills and other drugs.

Relax in the most natural ways possible, such as lying in the sun (apply a sunscreen lotion if your skin is fair) or taking warm baths.

Train members of your household to go along with your program, as well as to stock plenty of soft drinks.

Seek out wholesome entertainment that is not too sordid and heavy, such as comedies, light plays, inspiring stories, and books with positive themes.

Slow down and avoid trying to do too much.

Above all keep your lifestyle simple and live one day at a time.

(H) HOW, WHERE, AND WHEN TO SEEK OUTSIDE HELP

1. *Q.* What should be my first step if I have seriously tried to establish safe-drinking habits and attitudes and find that I am constantly slipping back into the old ways?

   A. The very first step is to take as much time as possible for an honest self-evaluation. Enlist the aid of relatives and friends who are close to you. The more information you can impart about your problems and failures, the more quickly you are likely to get the help you need. It's like going to your family doctor. If all you can tell him is that you get tired easily or have vague feelings of discomfort, he may be just as much at a loss as you are about the problem. But if you can zero in on certain aches and pains and symptoms, he may be able to put his finger on the trouble right away.

2. *Q.* Is my family doctor the one whom I should turn to first in a matter as delicate and specialized as drinking?

   A. Most physicians today, including general practitioners, are more knowledgeable about drinking problems than they were in the past. Even if your family physician does not feel qualified to advise you, he will know where to suggest that you go for help. Besides that, you should have a thorough physical examination by a doctor who knows you and has your medical history on file. There may be physiological imbalances or clues that will assist in further guidance.

3. *Q.* Where do I turn if I don't want to go to my private physician or I feel that he may not be knowledgeable enough?

   A. Get in touch with your local hospital and ask for alcohol information. In most cases, you will be referred to someone who can provide information about local specialists in this field. Ask to see the new AMSA directory that lists specialists in the field of alcohol.

   Q. But aren't most specialists interested in treating alcoholics? They might not want to waste time on someone who is not yet having major problems with alcohol.

   A. That is true to a certain extent. But one thing a specialist knows full well is that alcoholism is a disease and some people who have that disease may be in the earliest stages and hardly recognizable at all as problem drinkers. Doctors have to determine whether such persons *are* alcoholics or whether they are relatively normal drinkers who need proper counsel and possibly medical assistance. If a specialist feels that he is "over-qualified" for your particular type of drinking problem, he will refer you to someone else. It is better to reach a specialist with deep, broad experience than a generalist who may not understand your problem.

4. *Q.* Do all physicians consider alcoholism a disease?

A. Today, most people in the medical profession view alcoholism as a disease—just as much as they think of asthma or diabetes or hypertension as diseases. One of the ways you can determine whether your own family doctor, or any other physician, can be helpful with drinking problems is to ask him directly: "Do you consider alcoholism a disease?" If he hedges, or answers in the negative, he may not be as up to date in this field of medicine as he is in some other areas. The American Medical Association, American College of Psychiatrists, American Psychiatric Association, and other major associations in the field of medicine have all agreed that alcoholism *is* a disease and that it should be treated as such, and not as a moral problem.

5. *Q.* Are medical associations good sources of information about where to get help? If so, what ones would I find locally?

A. The following kinds of organizations are good ones to turn to, all of which can be found in your telephone directory, probably in the Yellow Pages:

The National Council on Alcoholism, with branches or affiliates in major locations across the United States. If you cannot locate a local branch, contact NCA headquarters, 12 West 21st Street, New York, NY 10010, (212) 206-6770.

Your county medical society

The state alcoholism division

The county Mental Health Board

A major source of assistance, whether you contact any of the above agencies or not, is Alcoholics Anonymous. Look for "AA" at the beginning of the phone book, as well as under the complete name. Many people shy away from calling AA, feeling, mistakenly, that it can only help "drunks." AA will make every effort to put you in contact with the right facility, if you explain your problem and your needs.

6. *Q.* What is Alcoholics Anonymous?
   A. AA is a fellowship of alcoholics who have admitted that they have problems with drinking and who derive a common identity, insight, and purpose from recognition of their inability to cope with their alcoholism. Members reinforce their abstinence through frequent meetings of local groups, at which they narrate their personal histories and constantly affirm their common creed, rules of conduct, and forms of service to other alcoholics. Members remain anonymous, using only their first names at meetings and refraining from any kind of outside publicity. They believe in total abstinence, that they must stay away from that first drink, one day at a time.

7. *Q.* Can AA help a person who is not an alcoholic

but who seriously wants to cut down on amounts
he drinks and change drinking habits?

A.   Most certainly. Calling an AA phone number will
put you in touch with other organizations, such
as a local branch of the National Council on Alcoholism, that can assist you in your need. AA will
also inform you about the dates and locations
of "open meetings" that are usually held once
a week by AA groups. These meetings are open
to the public, and anyone with drinking problems, large or small, is especially welcomed.
Meetings are casual. Coffee, soft drinks and
cookies are usually served. You can be as congenial or as reserved as you like. If you talk to
members or guests, you need simply introduce
yourself by your first name and retain complete
anonymity. You are in no way committed to anything. No one will try to sign you up or ask questions. The meetings usually consist of a moderator, an alcoholic, who will introduce two or three
speakers. The speakers, recovered alcoholics,
will relate some of their experiences with drinking and how they eventually achieved sobriety.
After the meeting, you can feel perfectly free
to talk with anyone on the program and ask questions about AA. If you feel that your own drinking has gotten completely out of hand, you can
find out where and when AA meetings are held.

8.   *Q.*   Suppose that I badly need help and am afraid
that I may have this disease of alcoholism myself,
how do I join AA and what are my obligations?

A.   All you have to do is to attend meetings regularly
and listen to what other people have to say about
alcohol, their drinking problems, and how they
succeeded or failed in past efforts to stay sober.

You do not "sign up," or make any form of commitment. You can attend meetings as often as you like—once a week, twice a week, once a day if you find it helpful. Remember, though, that the AA concept calls for total abstinence, "one day at a time." There is no plan for cutting down on drinking or learning how to ration your alcoholic consumption.

9. *Q.* What takes place at an AA meeting?

A. Members of that particular group usually arrive 5 or 10 minutes early, in time to have a cup of coffee or tea or a soft drink. Some engage each other in conversation; others will sit silently sipping coffee or reading some of the AA publications that are on a nearby table or rack. Newcomers are greeted casually and congenially by two or three regular members and every effort is made to put you at ease. You'd hear comments like these:

"Hi, I'm Sally. It's nice to see you here. Would you like some coffee or tea?"

"Hello. My name is Pete. I think you'll enjoy our group. We've been coming here about three years. And we've grown from six members to more than thirty now."

"Glad to see you. Make yourself at home and if you have any questions, just ask. I'm Bill."

Meetings are often held in a church, often in a basement room where there is a large table that people can sit around. One of the regular members opens the meeting and may make brief announcements about such matters as a special event of interest to the group, a new AA publication, or a scheduled TV broadcast on alcoholism. The moderator usually recounts personal battles with alcohol and calls on others to volunteer their stories and ways in which they have managed to stay sober and improve their lives. People who are new to AA will, over a period of attendance at meetings, identify with the catastrophes they themselves have experienced and begin finding answers to some of their drinking problems.

Q. What kinds of people would I meet at a typical AA meeting?

A. Membership is composed of people from every facet of life, old and young, married and single, covering most religious affiliations, professions, ethnic groups, and degrees of poverty or wealth.

10. *Q.* What do I do if someone I love has a drinking problem and is badly in need of help?

A. The answer revolves around what we often call "intervention" in professional circles. Don't be phased by the term. It simply means that you take steps to *intervene,* or get the alcoholic to realize his or her problem and want to be helped.

Often alcoholics can be motivated by family groups who force them to face the problems that are affecting the whole families and all whose lives are closely touched by the alcoholics.

Q. Doesn't this take a lot of skill and knowledge?

A. To some extent. But fortunately you can obtain a great deal of help and counseling. When you get down to it, there are two things you have to deal with. One is *denial* by alcoholics that there is nothing really wrong with their drinking. The other is that they will *manipulate,* connive, and even lie and deceive to try to keep from being challenged. Here is where loved ones can put into practice what we call "tough love." They confront their alcoholic, insist on the plain truth, and as a family group, make plans for getting the sick person into treatment. They do so out of love and the hope for recovery.

11. *Q.* All right, suppose I am ready to attempt this act of intervention, where do I turn?

A. To any of the agencies, or types of agencies mentioned earlier. If you have time, first write for a very valuable publication entitled "Alcoholism Intervention." It is *free* and can be obtained from: The Christopher D. Smithers Foundation, P.O. Box 67, Mill Neck, NY 11765.

This ten-page pamphlet provides sound, helpful information, describes the procedure, and advises you about seeking help.

12. *Q.* Besides AA and the various organizations you have mentioned that concern themselves with alcohol, do you have any other suggestions about sources of help?

A. One more is important, for people who have jobs with large corporations, who belong to unions or some of the professional associations, or who are on the payroll of the government, public utilities, and other large organizations of any kind. More and more of these organizations now have "EAPs," Employee Assistance Programs, that are particularly geared to helping people with drinking problems. If you are an employee, find out whether such a program is available. If so, you can expect a great deal of help, and at no cost to you.

Q. Why would I want to reveal that I have a drinking problem, and maybe run the risk of being fired on the spot?

A. If you do have a problem, you run less risk by

taking advantage of professional assistance within the organization than by trying to hide it. Employers have a great responsibility when they establish an EAP and are committed first and foremost to assisting all employees in the program and preserving their anonymity. Department heads and managers are not informed about participation by employees under their supervision, unless they themselves have initiated the action because of alcohol-related problems on the job.

A company EAP would be an effective alternative for people who are not alcoholics and who want to cut back on their drinking and cannot do it alone. Usually the medical department is closely involved with such a program and is well-equipped to counsel people who are slipping into unsafe drinking habits and who may have physiological problems that relate to their drinking, such as high blood pressure, gastrointestinal ailments, or overweight.

In some cases, especially where there are physiological problems that affect, or have been affected by, overindulgence in alcohol, a rehabilitation center is advised. A rehab center, usually associated with a hospital, is simply a place where patients can get proper rest, treatment, and counsel about alcohol-related problems and ailments.

Q. One final question. If I have a problem, or someone I love has a problem, just what do I say on the phone when calling one of these agencies for help? I'm not very good at this sort of thing.

A. Few people are. Yet it's quite simple because all of the agencies discussed are sympathetic, understanding, and quite accustomed to reassuring callers who may be embarrassed, tongue-tied, or both.

First, be perfectly *honest*. Don't try to make up some story about a "friend" who seems to be having this problem and how you'd like to help out. If *you* have the problem, say so. If you want help for a loved one, say so.

Make it short, simple, and to the point. "I have a drinking problem. I'm losing control and may be an alcoholic. I'd like to get help as soon as possible . . ." Then let the person at the other end of the line take over.

Don't forget, these agencies realize that alcoholism is an *illness*. They will treat your call in the same understanding manner as though you had phoned your doctor to report that you had a severe sore throat and fever.

To sum it all up, the consumption of alcoholic beverages causes few problems for nine out of ten people. If alcohol is used moderately and with respect by people who are normal drinkers, it has the potential to be a pleasurable part of socializing, sharing good food and friendship, and celebrating special occasions.

If, however, the use of alcohol leads to problems with one's health, job, family, or personal relationships, it is important to recognize that the problems can be successfully overcome with appropriate treatment and a sympathetic, nonpunitive attitude.